MAY MORRIS

MAY MORRIS

ARTS *&* CRAFTS DESIGNER

ANNA MASON, JAN MARSH, JENNY LISTER, ROWAN BAIN AND HANNE FAURBY

WITH CONTRIBUTIONS BY ALICE MCEWAN AND CATHERINE WHITE

FOREWORD BY LYNN HULSE

Thames &Hudson | V&A | WM WILLIAM MORRIS GALLERY

To Linda Parry, with thanks and appreciation

COVER
Front: 'Spring and Summer' panel (detail),
designed and probably embroidered by
May Morris, 1895–1900. Private collection.
Back: May Morris, 1908, photograph by
George Charles Beresford. Photo © The
William Morris Gallery, London Borough of
Waltham Forest, WMG (P644)

FRONTISPIECE
May Morris working on embroidery,
early 1890s
Unknown photographer
National Portrait Gallery (NPG x44650)

Note
Dimensions of works are given in centimetres and inches, height before width,
unless stated otherwise.

Published in association with the exhibition 'May Morris: Art and Life'
William Morris Gallery, London
7 October 2017 – 28 January 2018

First published in the United Kingdom in 2017 by
Thames & Hudson, 181A High Holborn, London WC1V 7QX
in association with the Victoria and Albert Museum, London

First published in the United States of America in 2017 by
Thames & Hudson Inc., 500 Fifth Avenue, New York, New York 10110

First paperback edition published in 2022

Reprinted 2023

May Morris: Arts & Crafts Designer © 2017 Victoria and Albert Museum,
London/Thames & Hudson
Text and V&A photographs © 2017 Victoria and Albert Museum, London
Design © 2017 Thames & Hudson

Designed by Peter Dawson, Alice Kennedy-Owen, www.gradedesign.com

British Library Cataloguing-in-Publication Data
A catalogue record for this book is available from the British Library

Library of Congress Control Number 2017934765

ISBN 978-0-500-48081-6

Printed in China by Shenzhen Reliance Printing Co. Ltd

Be the first to know about our new releases,
exclusive content and author events by visiting
thamesandhudson.com
thamesandhudsonusa.com
thamesandhudson.com

V&A Publishing
Supporting the world's leading
museum of art and design,
the Victoria and Albert
Museum, London

CONTENTS

FOREWORD

LYNN HULSE

Overshadowed by the achievements of her more illustrious father, the contribution of May Morris (1862–1938) to the decorative arts, in particular to art embroidery, of the later nineteenth and early twentieth centuries has in the past received less attention from scholars and curators than it deserves. It is now thirty years since Jan Marsh's biography, followed by the first retrospective exhibition of her life and work at the William Morris Gallery in 1989. Since then and especially since the millennium, research has greatly extended knowledge and interpretation. May's biography has been updated, and several facets of her long career as designer and maker have been discussed in new studies of the Arts and Crafts movement, notably in the revised edition of Linda Parry's seminal work, *William Morris Textiles* (2013). Royal Mail commemorated the 150th anniversary of her birth in 2012 in the 'Britons of Distinction' stamp collection, which featured *Orange Tree*, designed and embroidered by May around 1897.

Interest in May Morris's work has grown at a steady pace. In 2016, the William Morris Gallery hosted a two-day conference exploring new research; its proceedings are listed in the bibliography of this book, which is published to coincide with the exhibition 'May Morris: Art and Life' held at the Gallery in autumn 2017.

May Morris is recognized today as a leading figure in the Arts and Crafts movement. From the late 1890s she took up jewellery-making (a selection of her pieces is included in this book) but her enduring passion was decorative needlework, for which she continued to execute commissions until the final months of her life. Published here for the first time is *A Garden Piece*, designed and stitched by May in 1938, which epitomizes her love of English meadow plants and cottage garden flowers, a constant theme throughout her work.

May was a key exponent of art embroidery, the champions of which sought to overturn the Victorian obsession with Berlin work, a form of shading in cross stitch or tent stitch that lacked both manual dexterity and aesthetic subtlety; in so doing, art embroidery elevated needlework from a domestic craft to a serious art form. The earliest textbook on the subject, *Art Embroidery* (1878), asserted that '[t]he first condition of an ideal work of art is that it should be conceived and carried out by one person; division of labour is fatal to distinction and individuality'.[1] May Morris is the embodiment of that paradigm, and her output is testament to her creative skills both as designer and maker.

As an accomplished needlewoman, May also shared her parents' commitment to reviving historic stitch. Her comments on its development and technicality, born of in-depth study of old examples in museum collections and church treasuries across Britain and mainland Europe, rank her among the leading instructors in the field. In 1893, church architect and designer John Dando Sedding claimed that '[e]very ingenious stitch of old humanity has been mastered',[2] yet most art embroiderers, including May, employed a small vocabulary of stitches in the belief that '[e]xcellence of workmanship does not lie in many curious and difficult varieties of stitch, but in the expressive use of a few ordinary ones.'[3] May's work, both in the Morris & Co. house style and in the special commissions and gifts for family and friends designed and executed in her own distinctive manner, was created using only a handful of embroidery stitches, the chief examples of which are described in her guidebook *Decorative Needlework* (1893). Designs such as *Olive and Rose* or *Tulip* – worked primarily in darning stitch – demonstrate her artistry in interpreting naturalistic growth using a simple running stitch.

Technical skill alone was not sufficient. Invention, argued May, lay in the selection and arrangement of colours, the choice of suitable materials and, above all, good design based on an appreciation of the intellectual quality of English medieval embroidery, the apogee of needle-art. Taken together, these four elements ensured that a piece of embroidery 'shall not be meaningless, but rather a thing of use and individual interest'.[4]

Invention lies at the heart of the work discussed and illustrated in this book. Combined with ingenuity in the choice and application of stitch, it secures May's position in the pantheon of British designer-makers of the later nineteenth and early twentieth centuries, as her needlework continues to absorb and inspire today.

1

A Well-Crafted Life

JAN MARSH

PAGE 8

1

May Morris (far right) with
her parents, William and Jane
Morris, 1874 [detail of fig. 5]

FOR MORE THAN a century, the name and fame of William
Morris has eclipsed and indeed obscured the career of his daughter May
Morris, leading designer and maker in the Arts and Crafts movement.

May Morris's works exemplify the first principle of the Arts and
Crafts movement, that the design and making of an object be by the
same person, in a craft process both aesthetic and practical. Those
shown here reveal the breadth, variety and originality of her designs
and the quality of the craft skill that created individual pieces.

May Morris was born on 25 March 1862 – in traditional terms Lady
Day or the feast of the Annunciation. She was therefore named 'Mary',
immediately transformed into 'May'. Her birthplace was Red House, in
Bexley, Kent, then a rural, fruit-growing area, now part of the sprawling
London conurbation. She had a sister, Jenny, just fifteen months older,
and her parents were Jane Burden Morris, daughter of a stableman,
and William Morris, a wealthy, university-educated young man with
a passion for art, literature and all things medieval, who would become
a famous poet, designer, businessman and political activist [figs 1–3].
Designed by his friend Philip Webb, brick-built Red House is now
regarded as a landmark building of the Victorian age, heralding Arts
and Crafts domestic architecture.

Around the time of May's birth, her father, who was a man of sudden
but always creative passions, launched a small-scale business, designing
and making items for ecclesiastical and domestic use along traditional
methods. The products included stained glass, painted furniture, wall
decorations, metalwork, painted tiles, wallpaper and embroidered
textiles, later expanding into printed and woven fabrics, including
tapestry and carpets. From the beginning, the needlecraft items were
made by Jane Morris, her sister Elizabeth (Bessie) Burden, and friends
within the Morrises' social circle – sisters Kate and Lucy Faulkner,
Georgiana Burne-Jones and Catherine Holiday.

May therefore grew up in an environment of intensive craftwork.
From 1865 the family lived in Queen Square, central London, alongside
the glass-painting workshop, and from an early age May and Jenny
stitched simple items such as pen-wipers and kettle-holders, while their
mother and aunt embroidered altar cloths, wall hangings, coverlets,
cushions and fire screens, as well as book covers and clothing. The
business, from 1875 known as Morris & Co., then employed embroidery
outworkers supervised by Jane and aunt Bessie, and had a showroom
in Oxford Street, where a full range of decorative schemes could be
ordered. William Morris insisted on studying and practising, albeit
on a small scale, all the processes used for the firm's products, from
calico printing to dyeing yarn, from framing stained-glass panels to
knotting carpets, using many pre-industrial methods and demanding
high quality. He was more opposed to the poor results of mass
production than committed to hand work for its own sake, but May
inherited from him a devotion to meticulous craft practice that was
in line with single pieces rather than machine-made batches.

'I am a great tomboy', wrote May in a 'description of myself' aged 8.
'I am very untidy and always very dirty and sometimes I am ashamed
to say very naughty. I have got light curly hair cut on my forehead.
My eyes are blue. I am neither fat nor very thin.'[1] May and her sister
had an unconventional upbringing, enjoying more active pursuits
than were commonly allowed for girls, especially at the family's
summer home from 1871, Kelmscott Manor in Oxfordshire, an
unspoilt Cotswold stone building of the sixteenth and seventeenth
centuries where one room retained antique tapestry hangings.

Around were fields and paddocks to explore and there was a punt on the nearby river Thames. From 1878, the family's London home was Kelmscott House at Hammersmith on the Thames riverside; here the firm's embroidery department was based, while the rest of the business moved to Merton in Surrey, on the river Wandle. In the 1890s, the last years of his life, William Morris set up the Kelmscott Press, producing finely designed, printed and bound books in a workshop such as Caxton himself might have managed.

Thanks to the artistic circles in which the Morrises moved, May and her sister were accustomed to sit for sketches and paintings. Pre-Raphaelite painter Dante Gabriel Rossetti – partner in the Morris firm, co-tenant of Kelmscott Manor and for a few years Jane Morris's close companion – was foremost among these, using May as a model for several pictures during the 1870s [fig. 7]. Other artists included Edward Burne-Jones, with whose wife and children the Morrises were especially close [fig. 5], and George Howard, later Earl of Carlisle, himself a painter, friend and customer of the Morris firm [figs 4, 6].

When William Morris began his experiments in dyeing silk and woollen yarn, May and her sister were given a set of dyestuffs to practise (or play) with. She long remembered 'the broad-stoppered bottles filled with queer powders and lumps and grains that stood on an inviting shelf in the schoolroom, and what distressing messes we made with them!' Later she assisted with colouring patterns for the firm's new rugs, recalling 'what a lot of raw umber

and Chinese white we used sometimes!' – the white being to correct mistakes – and noting how 'it was all fine workshop training for a young artist'.[2]

May's formal education took place at home, with a couple of years' secondary schooling that was curtailed after her sister Jenny developed epilepsy and Jane took her daughters to Italy, staying near to the Howards. In autumn 1878, May enrolled at the National Art Training School (later the Royal College of Art) in South Kensington, choosing embroidery as her specialism [fig. 8]. As part of her course, she studied medieval embroidery known as *opus anglicanum* (Latin for 'English work'), she also made watercolour records of ancient artworks, wild flowers and landscapes, a sketching habit that continued.

Aged just 23, in 1885 May took charge of the Morris & Co. embroidery department, at first in Kelmscott House and later in separate premises. The appointment indicates she was already regarded as a leading craftworker in the field, and in this role she produced embroidery designs for bespoke and stock items, supervised staff and young trainees recruited from local schools, and handled all orders, as itemized in the surviving volume of the firm's Day Book. Among the popular products were embroidery 'kits', the design traced onto fabric and part-stitched for completion by the customer.

ABOVE LEFT
6
Portrait sketch of May Morris by George Howard, Earl of Carlisle, 1870. From a sketchbook now at Wightwick Manor, Wolverhampton (NT 1288044)

ABOVE RIGHT
7
Pastel study of May Morris by Dante Gabriel Rossetti, 1871. Drawn at Kelmscott Manor when May was aged 9. Society of Antiquaries of London (KM060)

OPPOSITE
8
May Morris, aged 17, by an unidentified photographer. Taken around the time she studied at the National Art Training School in South Kensington. WMG (P641)

For Morris & Co., May also designed wallpaper patterns, which, like the textiles, were in the 'house style'. *Honeysuckle* has proved most enduring, becoming one of the firm's ever-popular designs.

At the same time as managing the embroidery workshop, May was drawn into political activity in the emergent Socialist movement. Alongside Eleanor Marx, George Bernard Shaw, the activist Annie Besant and future prime minister Ramsay MacDonald, she experienced a ferment of radical idealism. May and her friends were also passionate about the New Drama with its exploration of social and personal struggles, staging some of the first performances of Henrik Ibsen's plays in Britain. May herself acted in amateur performances, wrote two short plays, and was in demand as a musician, playing piano and guitar [fig. 11].

One of May's contemporaries described her personality as 'fire and ice' – warmly passionate in favour and frosty in disapproval. Her surviving letters – and a newly discovered valentine – to Bernard Shaw display assertive wit unusual for young women of the time. She and Shaw fell in love, but when he insisted he was too poor to marry – before he found fame and fortune as a playwright – she replied with dignified candour: 'I don't think our intercourse can have caused you more pleasure than it has me', adding: 'I have always been most impatient of the bourgeois vulgarity of thought and the attendant convention which almost entirely prevents young men and women from holding that frank and friendly intercourse without which life

ABOVE

9

From left: May Morris; her husband-to-be Henry (Harry) Sparling; process engraver Emery Walker; critic and later playwright George Bernard Shaw, rehearsing for a Socialist League entertainment, *c.* 1886. Cheltenham Museum and Art Gallery

May Morris on 22 March 1886,
shortly before her 24th birthday.
Photograph by Frederick Hollyer.
WMG (P665)

With love from May Morris

is nothing to my mind. Let us be comrades by all means – I salute you,
friend Shaw!'[3]

Thus emotionally rebuffed, May turned to another Socialist named
Henry Halliday Sparling, whom she married in 1890. The marriage
was short-lived, however, ending in divorce in 1899. The Socialist
excitement of the period was similarly brief, eclipsed for many by
the reforming Liberal government of 1906 and then by the angry
Suffragette campaign when reform failed to include the franchise.

In many ways May Morris exemplified the New Woman of
1890–1910, with freedom of movement, independent choices and
egalitarian pursuits, but also a certain loneliness owing to conservative

attitudes towards single women. While lending her skills to the women's movement, she did not join Suffragette actions, believing that socialism was more important than gender disadvantage.

Professionally, May's career advanced in step with the Arts and Crafts movement, which in Britain emerged during the 1880s, in reaction against decorative elaboration and mechanized manufacture. Inspired by the polemical writing of John Ruskin, castigating the dehumanization of labour, it recognized William Morris as a founding father, thanks to his promotion of traditional methods. Arts and Crafts principles included a belief in truth to material, structure and function. It favoured simple forms, motifs from nature and vernacular art, and well-made items for use rather than display. Architecture and interior design were major elements in the movement – hence Morris's famous dictum to 'have nothing in your houses that you do not know to be useful or believe to be beautiful'. Dress also featured, in the form of simple clothing, sometimes made from hand-woven fabrics and worn with hand-crafted jewellery.

The movement fostered the individual craftsperson, usually working along traditional lines, alone or in small workshops. From 1888, the Arts & Crafts Exhibition Society held regular shows in London [fig. 13]. As the artist Walter Crane, its first president, explained: 'We desired first of all to give opportunity to the designer and craftsman to exhibit their work to the public for its artistic interest and thus to assert the claims of decorative art and handicraft to attention equally with the painter of easel pictures, hitherto almost exclusively associated with the term art in the public mind.' The belief, he added, was that 'everything depended upon the spirit as well as the skill and fidelity with which the conception was expressed, in whatever material, seeing that a worker earned the title of artist by the sympathy with and treatment of his [*sic*] material, by due recognition of its capacity, and its natural limitations, as well as of the relation of the work to use and life.'[4]

The Society flourished until the First World War curtailed its activities, and it was eventually succeeded by today's Society of Designer Craftsmen. May Morris was a regular exhibitor and contributor to Arts and Crafts publications. While never claiming a leadership role, she became a central figure in the movement, as designer, maker and teacher. She wrote warmly of Crane as the 'most picturesque' and of the architect W. R. Lethaby as 'the most scholarly and practical' member of the movement, and throughout her career commended the study of 'good work of past times', based on 'simple rules…so simple that "anybody" could learn how, if they wanted to!'[5]

Committed to the integration of design and making, she wrote that '[i]n modern decorative work the estrangement between designer and

OPPOSITE

11

May Morris at Kelmscott House, playing the guitar. Photograph probably by Emery Walker, *c.* 1886. WMG (P652)

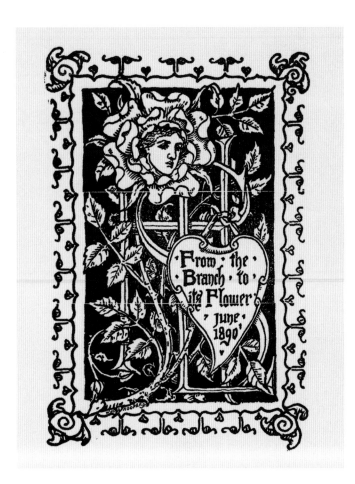

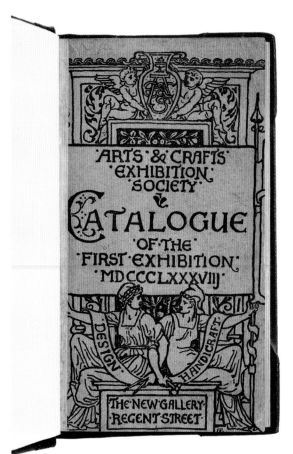

executant generally creates a want of unity and coherence' because '[t]he designer frequently has no full knowledge of the materials and tools employed, and his drawings, made independently…lose force or delicacy in execution; while the craftsman loses the knowledge he formerly possessed of the value of line and masses, as he is no longer, as a rule, called upon to think and create in his work – a disastrous division of labour, with disastrous results.'[6]

In 1899, in a paper to the International Congress of Women in London, May analysed the contemporary field of embroidery. 'First, we have the amateur who works at home; on the other hand, there is the young woman who must make a living, and seeks what she calls "light work" and, however honest and faithfully she does her daily task, yet it is a task. She does not have to think or invent much; her intelligence is only exercised mechanically, and her greatest interest is in the task's wage.' In addition, there were Church schools, which regrettably 'do not now produce the interesting work they once did' and 'a few philanthropic work societies, some of which, in finding employment for women, make it distinctly understood that none but gentlewomen "by birth and education" need apply – a restriction which rather narrows the scope of such enterprises.'

ABOVE LEFT

12

'From the Branch to its Flower', 1890, woodcut bookplate designed by Walter Crane and engraved by W. H. Hooper to accompany a wedding gift to May of books from the Hammersmith Branch of the Socialist League, with a message signed by thirty members saying, 'You have lived among us and have worked for us with your best strength'. WMG (P807)

ABOVE RIGHT

13

'Arts & Crafts Exhibition Society', 1888, cover designed by Walter Crane for the catalogue of the first exhibition. WMG (K1027)

Lastly, there were those few 'who, furnished with a historical
knowledge for the art, happen to have leisure and opportunity
to pursue it experimentally on new and unwonted lines. Their
experiments may succeed or fail, but their work has always some
note of interest, in so far as it is thoughtful, and embodies the serious
effort and training for which all art imperatively calls.'[7] May herself
belonged to this innovative category [fig. 14].

In respect of her chosen field, May's career falls into distinct phases.
From graduation to the death of her father in 1896, she was chiefly
occupied with designing for and managing the Morris & Co. workroom,
exhibiting both with the firm and on her own account. Her designs
followed the 'Morris style' that was the firm's hallmark and patterns
such as *Honeysuckle* have been mistaken for her father's. However, as
noted by textile historian Linda Parry, who pioneered the study and
revaluation of May Morris's career, where William Morris designs
incorporated motifs like pomegranates and acanthus, May favoured
English hedgerow and meadow plants, often based on her own botanical
drawings. Her work also reflected historical knowledge, style and
stitching including references to earlier crewel work, fine eighteenth-
century silk and beadwork, or folkloric patterning, as appropriate.

Her own items were produced to commission, or as gifts for family and friends. From 1897, she taught embroidery practice and design, at the Central School of Arts and Crafts, under W. R. Lethaby, at Birmingham School of Art, where her friend Mary Newill was the instructor, and at Hammersmith Art School. As such she was the first of a new group of instructors who encouraged the teaching of complex historic techniques in order to revive 'the manual dexterity, skills and knowledge…that formed the basis of craft teaching throughout the first half of the twentieth century and provided a legacy that is still at the heart of art education today'.[8] This period saw the creation of many exceptional pieces, including large door curtains and bed hangings worked in wools on linen and stunning panels in silk on silk damask where strong subtle colours glow with a soft sheen, and the eye follows sinuous patterns of foliage, birds and lettering. These are among the masterpieces illustrated in this book.

Embroidered book covers and bindings form a subsection in May's *oeuvre*, while needlecrafts were later augmented by jewellery and metalwork, mainly in silver and with cabochon stones in the Arts and Crafts mode. These items featured with embroidery in two modest exhibitions, in London in 1905 and New York in 1910. Following visits to Orkney and Mallorca [fig. 16], May added spinning and weaving to her craft skills, and later also began tapestry weaving [fig. 22].

On a lengthy lecture tour of North America in 1909–10, May shared her extensive historical knowledge of embroidered textiles and techniques [fig. 17]. In print she also expressed very personal tastes, such as her liking for the colour blue – 'one of the pleasantest to have constantly under one's eye'. Hence her advice:

> Of blue choose those shades that have the pure, slightly grey tone of indigo dye…it is neither slatey nor too hot, nor too cold, nor does it lean to that unutterably coarse green-blue, libellously called 'peacock' blue; it has different tones – brilliant sometimes, and sometimes quiet – reminding one now of the grey-blue of a distant landscape, and now of the intense blue of a midday summer sky – if anything can resemble that.[9]

Most significantly, in 1907 she founded the Women's Guild of Arts, for those working on an independent basis in arts and crafts of all kinds. This was in explicit compensation for exclusion from the social and professional networking of the existing Art Workers' Guild, which did not admit its first female member until 1972. She outlined WGA objectives as follows:

OPPOSITE

15
Portrait drawing of May Morris
by Mary Annie Sloane, *c.* 1900.
Mary Sloane (1867–1961) was
May's close friend and colleague
in the Women's Guild of Arts.
In 1923, she took over the lease
of May's home in Hammersmith
Terrace. WMG (D277)

ABOVE

16

May Morris in Soller, Mallorca, July 1913. Photograph probably taken by Mary Sloane. University of Delaware, Mark Samuels Lasner Collection

As I understand it, we are a body of women joined together as such, men always having their own organisation, to do what we are doing i.e. to keep to the highest level the arts by which and for which we live, to keep ever fresh and vital the enthusiasm, the belief – all the things which are the impetus of human endeavour. Perhaps also we have the mission of heartening up the weary (among whom may sometimes be ourselves and each other in times of trouble and depression) and generally of exuding an atmosphere of camaraderie without which one's work would surely be as Dead Sea fruit.[10]

The parenthesis is revealing: women working in the craft field often felt isolated and unsupported. As the Guild records show, several notable artists were fellow-members, the first president being Mary Seton Watts, wife of the painter G. F. Watts RA and herself active in ceramic and architectural design. Others included painters Evelyn de Morgan and Marie Stillman, jeweller Georgie Gaskin, bookbinder Katharine Adams and sculptor Mabel White. The Guild showcased members' work and hosted discussions; its atmosphere is conveyed in May's account of a day in December 1910, when Mary Newill came to lunch:

An accomplished charming woman, and we had great talks. Then two other women came – all of us members of my Woman's Guild – and there we were, talking of the Post-Impressionists, of the last new way of teaching art students – of shop in short…I must say it was as fine a little knot of women with an all-round, not self-centred, view of the arts as you could meet anywhere; all comely, well-grown creatures, bubbling with vitality and good humour… It is a pleasure to meet women who know their work and are not playing at art.[11]

(May incidentally responded more favourably than many to the Post-Impressionist show in London in 1910, admiring Paul Cézanne, Vincent van Gogh and especially Paul Gauguin, whose 'extraordinary experiments with green skies, scarlet trees [and] dream-like foregrounds with pre-historic wriggling growths' contained 'wild snatches of poetry, even of sentiment…I am afraid this is all rank heresy'.[12])

A high point in the Arts and Crafts movement came with May's involvement in the great decorative arts exhibitions organized under British government auspices and shown in Belgium and France in 1913 and 1914 respectively. She was a member of the consultative committee,

OUTLINES OF LECTURES

JEWELS

❡ The mystery of precious stones. Their properties: myth, magic and poetry. Chats from Pliny—A Roman lady's jewel-box. ❡ Late Greek and Roman work in the British Museum. Imperial Jewels: the Golden Crown at Vienna, the Silver Crown, the Iron Crown. The Sword of Charlemagne; Alfred's Jewel. Mediæval Jewels, French and English. St. Louis' Brooch; the Reliquaire Haricot, etc. How the Jewels were worn. ❡ Jewels of the 16th and 17th centuries, Italian and English. Beatrice D'Este; Mary of Lorraine, etc. "Jewels for all time"; the relation of the beautiful ornament to the beautiful face.

MEDIÆVAL EMBROIDERY

❡ The word-painting of the old romance-writers. The Gothic Spirit. ❡ Domestic Embroidery. Brilliant descriptions in testaments and inventories. Edward, the Black Prince; the Clothes of Richard II., etc. ❡ Church vestments. World-renowned English Embroidery in the 13th Century: Opus Anglicanum. The different Italian style. ❡ Mediæval work-shops and craft-guilds: rules and fines; names of the workers. A King's embroiderer and varlet. ❡ Technique of the old work. ❡ Famous Copes: The Ascoli Cope; the Syon Cope, the Pienza Cope, etc.

PAGEANTRY AND THE MASQUE

❡ PASSION PLAYS. Description of the pageant-wagons and their order. The Coventry plays. ❡ POPULAR PAGEANTS AND ROYAL PROGRESSES: the King's entry into his good city of London. A contrast: The Lord Mayor's show to-day and the entry of Richard II. into London. ❡ THE TRIUMPHS OF EMPEROR MAXIMILIAN. ❡ CORONATION OF ANNE BOLEYN. Hans Holbein. The Jousts at Westminster. ❡ The later COURT MASQUE. Ben Jonson's Masque of Queens. Inigo Jones. ❡ Conclusion: Petrarch's Triumphs.

Civic Forum Lecture Bureau   23 West 44th Street
WILLIAM B. FEAKINS, Secretary   Telephone: Bryant, 4897
NEW YORK

*Yours very truly
May Morris.*

headed by Crane, contributed the essay 'La Broderie' to the catalogues of both exhibitions, and lent a significant number of items (in Paris, 32 out of over 1,600 exhibits), as well as featuring as designer or executant of twenty pieces.[13] She was also responsible for selecting items for the 'Morris & Co.' room as part of the exhibition.

Another major undertaking in this period was the editorship of twenty-four volumes of her father's literary output, published as the *Collected Works of William Morris* (1910–15), with biographical introductions [fig. 21] to rectify what were felt to be deficiencies in the official 'life' of William Morris by J. W. Mackail (1899). With other acts, this helped secure his legacy, although today Morris is known and admired primarily for his design work and political ideas, rather than for poetry. May also took responsibility for the care of her widowed mother, who died in 1914, and of her incapacitated sister Jenny, who lived until 1935 [fig. 18]. Their father's will left the family estate in trust; for the rest of her life May had an assured but not lavish income, managed by trustees on her behalf.

During the First World War May divided her time between Hammersmith in London and Kelmscott in Oxfordshire. In London she organized some 'small Arts and Crafts shows, partly to help artists badly hit [by war], partly to keep those sort of things in view – as art and what it keeps alive mustn't go down the wind at this juncture'.[14] She volunteered at a munitions canteen, made garments for Belgian

ABOVE

18

May (far left) with her mother, sister Jenny and Ada Culmer, Jenny's nurse-companion, seated outside Kelmscott Manor, *c.* 1905. Cabinet card photograph by Carter & Co, Bristol. WMG (P693)

refugees and sent barrels of fruit to naval vessels. In the country she supervised the completion of 'some expensive and beautiful cottage-building'[15] in memory of her mother, assisted local families through the new Women's Institute and offered needlework instruction to village girls. On a daily basis, May lived a frugal, self-sufficient life, without extravagance or parsimony, yet with a distinct taste for quality and refinement. Kelmscott Manor had no electricity, piped water or central heating, and when there May travelled by pony cart or bicycle, writing of the exhilaration of cycling home in wind and rain or under a starry sky.

She befriended a Land Girl of Cornish ancestry named Mary Frances Vivian Lobb, who remained with May after the war, and whom she described as 'housekeeper, cook and companion, and I may add, my almoner'[16] – that is the person in charge of May's welfare, who was moreover devoted to her [fig. 20]. The couple undertook memorable visits to Iceland, travelling in William Morris's footsteps [fig. 19]. Of the last, in 1931, when she was 69, May wrote: 'I'm too old to be riding about in the Icelandic deserts, but it is very exciting.'[17]

'The house is damp', wrote one young visitor in 1925 (when May was 63), noting the piano raised on stilts in case of floods.

> But it is most beautiful and nearly everything in it is beautiful. The little dining room is hung with a very faded 'strawberry-thief' pattern; we had tea there, Miss Morris pouring out lovely china tea. The cake she made herself…her hair is grey and she is very fair, a sort of ice-fairy queen. She was wearing a charming white coat and blouse, yellow beads and a homespun white shirt with a blue and yellow striped pattern.[18]

'All May's days at Kelmscott were busy days', recalled Una Fielding, a young neurologist and distant cousin, describing the daily routine in the last decade:

> She got up about 8 and breakfasted with Miss Lobb. In warm weather all meals, even breakfast, were served under the verandah in the kitchen courtyard. Visitors always had breakfast in bed, with permission to smoke. About 9.30 she made a round of the garden for flowers then went on into the kitchen garden to select the vegetables for the day. Then came work – writing or sewing till lunch time. The two girls from the village who came each day to do the housework had lunch with us except on the rare occasions when there were visitors for this meal. After lunch there was coffee and halva and Russian cigarettes and talk. Then followed an afternoon session of writing or designing for some serious job of needlework. In the afternoons, especially in holiday time, people often came to see the house and May usually liked to take them round herself.[19]

ABOVE

21

May Morris in the Tapestry Room, Kelmscott Manor, 1912, watercolour by Mary Annie Sloane. May is shown checking her edition of her father's *Collected Works*, with galley proofs covering the table. Her spinning wheel is by the window. WMG (W158)

May Morris seated by a tapestry loom, in a photograph taken at Kelmscott Manor in 1920. Tapestry is worked from the back using a mirror (seen hanging on the left). National Portrait Gallery (NPG x1105)

Through the postwar period May lent her skills to preserving her father's legacy, supporting attempts to save Red House (it passed into National Trust care over sixty years later), and to constructing a village hall in Kelmscott [fig. 23]. Her chosen architect, Ernest Gimson, shared Arts and Crafts principles, and the style of May's memorial building was Cotswold vernacular. Always active in promoting the fine crafts, she supported their role in education and manufacturing, with a belief in access to decorative art practice for all in a democratic society. In 1936, she published two hefty volumes of her father's writing on political, social and artistic topics, and she welcomed Socialists and sympathetic visitors to the Manor.

Writing to Bernard Shaw at this date, she assessed her life in negative terms, but allowed herself a small boast, all the more notable for being uncharacteristic. Thinking back to her younger days, occupied equally with Socialist activity, theatre-going and managing the embroidery business, she wrote: 'I'm a remarkable woman – always was, though none of you seemed to think so.'[20]

May Morris died in October 1938, almost exactly forty-two years after her father. The villagers lined the road as the coffin was carried

MORRIS MEMORIAL HALL

KELMSCOTT, OXFORDSHIRE

EAST ELEVATION OF PROPOSED HALL

WILLIAM MORRIS is known throughout the world as the great poet who brought back to English literature the magic of Chaucer that had slept for five hundred years. But Kelmscott will not let it be forgotten that he did other work as well: handiwork such as was once done in English villages, and will be done there again because of him. His work as a decorative artist has passed into the substance of artistic consciousness and moulds every effort of to-day; his activities as a printer are apparent in every piece of good book-work in England, America, and Germany, however different in aim and form; while his social teaching has not only been the inspiration, directly or indirectly, of working-class leaders to-day, but has helped to mould the policies of all parties. And yet only in Kelmscott can those who knew him say, 'Here William Morris was at home.'

It has therefore been thought that in Kelmscott a memorial should be raised to his memory, beautiful in itself and useful to

LEFT

23

Fundraising appeal for a community hall in Kelmscott in memory of William Morris, 1928. May commissioned Arts and Crafts architect Ernest Gimson to design a simple Cotswold-style building and the hall opened in 1934 to mark the centenary of her father's birth. WMG (J906xxxviii)

on a farm wagon pulled by a great shire horse to the family grave in Kelmscott churchyard [fig. 24]. Her will safeguarded the family's culturally significant possessions, with bequests of art and craft works to the V&A and Ashmolean museums and manuscripts to what is now the British Library. The Society of Antiquaries – then the main heritage body – was residuary legatee, and requested to use the assets for architectural conservation. Her remaining possessions at the Manor were auctioned in July 1939, on the eve of the Second World War, which effectively eclipsed any immediate memorial.

May's artistic reputation also suffered subsequently, partly owing to the downgrading of embroidery as a purely female craft and partly to its inherent fragility, impacting on conservation and display. Although during the postwar years handcrafts continued to feature as part of public education, May Morris's significant role in the Arts and Crafts movement was largely forgotten until towards the end of the twentieth century, when both the fine crafts and the heritage values of the movement returned to study and practice.

ABOVE

24

May Morris's funeral,
Kelmscott village, October 1938.
Photograph by the *Evening
Advertiser*, Swindon. The coffin
was carried on a farm cart
from Kelmscott Manor to the
Morris family grave in the village
churchyard. WMG (PhJ911)

As Linda Parry wrote in 1996, the popularity cult that surrounds
William Morris led to the neglect of other individuals, notably May.
Mary Lobb spelled it out in a forthright manner to the director of
the V&A a month after May's death:

> You see William Morris could design embroideries but he could not
> embroider, anyway not as well…Mrs Morris could embroider but
> couldn't design, Miss Morris could and did both design as well as
> William Morris and embroider as well [as] any one…and her colour
> arrangements were unapproachable and original. To design, make
> and colour work which will hold its own and quite often far outstrip
> [others]…is what so few grasp and appreciate. They need to have
> their noses rubbed in it.[21]

May stands out among other art embroiderers of the late nineteenth
and early twentieth centuries as the ultimate exponent of the ideal of
the designer/craftswoman, conceiving and executing her own ideas, and
leaving a substantial body of work as evidence of her creative abilities.

2

Sketches and Watercolours

ROWAN BAIN

MAY'S SURVIVING SKETCHES and watercolours are now
scattered between various public and private collections. Distinct from
her professional output as a writer, teacher and designer, the works are
largely amateur in nature. They offer us, however, a proximity with
which to view more intimate aspects of her life, illustrating her deep
personal connection to her environment, including the houses she lived
in and the places and landscapes she enjoyed visiting. Largely free of
romanticism or sentimentality, the works reflect a determination to
record things as they were, and are a valuable account of the places that
influenced and shaped her life.

Like most middle-class girls in the nineteenth century, May began
painting and drawing during childhood. Yet her remarkable home
environment also meant she grew up amid her parents' successful artist
and designer friends. Such exposure, in which creative expression was
valued above all things, encouraged May's artistic talents. Close in age,
the Morris daughters were frequently distinguished by those who knew
them as the writer and artist, 'has not Jenny become a bard or May
painted a picture yet?' Dante Gabriel Rossetti asked Jane Morris in
1880.[1] This early distinction has endured as a way to describe the two
sisters' characters and although it overlooks Jenny's aptitude for
embroidery and May's intellectual abilities, as evidenced through her
teaching and writing, May's prodigious artistic output, which includes
watercolours, drawings and designs, leaves no doubt of her creative
talent in this regard.

May's earliest illustrations depict Kelmscott Manor, country retreat
of the family. Although May's drawings are now some of the earliest
surviving depictions of the Manor, even earlier is Rossetti's painting
Water Willow of 1871, in which Jane Morris is set against the background
of Kelmscott.[2] As an adult May recalled how his painting 'bothered me

ABOVE

26

Turin, from a sketchbook
of views in Italy and England
May Morris, 1884–85
Pencil, watercolour, woven
paper, leather and cloth
18.9 x 26.1 x 1.4 (7 ¹/₂ x 10 ¹/₄ x ¹/₂)
V&A (E.210–1942) Given by Sir
William Rothenstein

to have both house and church and boathouse all brought together
when they were in different directions. I confided to my mother my
doubts as to the morality of this, and demanded an explanation.
But the child's "This isn't how things really are!" can't be met by
explanation.'³ Although dismissed by May as a childish viewpoint, her
objections resound through her sketches and watercolours, which show
attempts to record accurately the Manor as it was. The faithful precision
with which she captured the many aspects and architectural details
of the house reflects the deep affection all members of the Morris
family had for the Manor, and her own desire to preserve and capture
its historic beauty [figs 30, 34].

William Morris and Rossetti jointly held the tenancy of Kelmscott
between 1871 and 1874, during the height of Rossetti's affair with Jane.
For two months during the summer of 1871, Jane and her daughters
lived with Rossetti at the Manor. May never openly wrote about the
complicated nature of this domestic arrangement or the conflict of
loyalty towards her father it must have evoked. Instead she wrote
sympathetically of the troubled artist who appeared fond of her and
encouraged her artistic talent. In her introduction to the *Collected Works*,
she later modestly alluded to how 'the slight aptitude for drawing
I was considered to have interested him'.⁴ The same passage describes
spending long hours modelling for Rossetti's paintings, staring at
the seventeenth-century tapestries depicting the story of Samson
and Delilah on the walls of the room, which she later painted in
a watercolour around 1880 [fig. 29].

May's formal education at Notting Hill High School for Girls was
brief, but the newly opened school was ambitious for its pupils and
expected many of them to progress into tertiary education. Jenny,
a keen student, passed the Cambridge Local Examination and but for
developing epilepsy would likely have gone to university. May instead

enrolled at the National Art Training School in South Kensington in 1878.

The new term started in October when May was 16 years old. However, life as a day-pupil at the Training School was far removed from the more modern notion of a bohemian art school. Lessons ran from nine in the morning and until a bell rang at 3.30, with just half an hour for lunch. The School occupied the north side of the present Victoria and Albert Museum, with separate studios for the 300 male and 400 female students.[5] The School was not only physically linked to the Museum, the two were institutionally aligned in providing training in the field of industrial design, the School's aim being specifically to prepare 'men and women who mean to earn their living as designers, or teachers of art students in schools throughout the country'.[6] At this period, art education in England was experiencing a rapid rise in popularity and many art training schools opened around the country; indeed May herself would teach at some, including Birmingham and Leicester.

During the years May studied at the National Art Training School its principal was Edward Poynter, who ran it from 1875 to 1881. Previously head of the Slade School of Art, he made drawing and painting from the live model foundational for art education, arguing that women students, like their male counterparts, should be taught in front of the nude figure. Appointed to the Training School, Poynter criticized its teaching methods, which allowed students to spend months working on 'drawings from the antique which had already occupied them a considerable portion of the previous term (five months), and were not half-finished'.[7] Poynter's methods may have influenced May's approach to design, observing natural forms in her botanical sketches before incorporating them into her finished designs [figs 41, 42].

ABOVE
27
A View of Kelmscott Manor
from across the Garden
May Morris, c. 1880
Watercolour on paper
25 x 36.5 (9⅞ x 14⅜)
National Trust, Wightwick Manor
(NT 1288006) Purchased by
Sir Geoffrey and Lady Mander
from the Kelmscott Manor sale
July 1939

OPPOSITE
28
View of Kelmscott Manor
from the Old Barn
May Morris, early 1880s
Paper and watercolour on paper
20 x 24 (7⅞ x 9½)
WMG (D294iii) Purchased by
Mr and Mrs Harmer Brown
from the Kelmscott Manor
sale July 1939

ABOVE

29
The Tapestry Room, Kelmscott
Manor
May Morris, early 1880s
Pencil and watercolour on paper
12.8 x 17.5 (5 x 6 7/8)
WMG (D294xi) Purchased by
Mr and Mrs Harmer Brown
from the Kelmscott Manor
sale July 1939

Although May exhibited many examples of her professional embroidery work, there is no record of her publicly showing her watercolours – a decision which reflects that she regarded herself as an amateur in this field. Most surviving sketches were kept for private enjoyment, only coming to notice following the sale at Kelmscott Manor in 1939, where they were dispersed among public and private collections. They include examples of watercolour sketches from her camping trips and expeditions to Iceland between 1924 and 1931 [figs 43, 44].[8]

Seen as a whole, the body of work is a testament to the personal enjoyment she gained from painting and sketching and one she clearly retained throughout her life.

30

Kelmscott Manor

May Morris, summer 1877

Ink on paper

23.4 × 37.5 (9 1/4 × 14)

WMG (D408) Given by Effie Morris, 1954

This small ink drawing is the earliest known surviving sketch by May, produced when she was just 15 years old. The assured lines and accuracy with which she captures the view of Kelmscott Manor reveal a young artistic talent. The view depicts the Manor from the rear, as seen from the paddock to its south. The trees are shown in full leaf, suggesting she sketched the drawing during the summer, when her family typically escaped their London home in Hammersmith to the rural peace of Oxfordshire. Kelmscott Manor was a subject she was to return to many times in her art. **RB**

Kelmscott Manor.

1877.

31

Villa della Cava

May Morris, inscribed 'November 1877'

Pencil on paper

16 x 25.3 (6 1/4 x 10)

Ashmolean Museum (WA1941.108.25), 1941

May spent the winter of 1877–78 with Jane and Jenny in this house in Oneglia (now Imperia), on the Ligurian coast of Italy. The six-month trip, part-organized by George and Rosalind Howard, was intended to improve Jenny's health after developing epilepsy the previous year. May later described the house as a 'beautiful unspoilt corner on the Cornice Road'.[9] This pencil sketch was drawn shortly after their arrival. It reveals May's enjoyment of drawing from nature, as the villa is shown peeking out of the lush garden that fills most of the page. Evidently May was very productive during this period, as her father complained in a letter 'Why hasn't May written to me yet? Is she too busy drawing?'[10] **RB**

32

Naworth Castle

May Morris, July–August 1878

Bodycolour on paper

26.4 x 35.3 (10³/₈ x 13⁷/₈)

Society of Antiquaries of London:
Kelmscott Manor (KM219)

Naworth, a medieval castle in north
Cumbria, belonged to George and
Rosalind Howard, later Earl and Countess
of Carlisle, good friends of the Morris
family. The Howards invited Jane and her
daughters to stay in Italy with them in 1877
[see fig. 31] and the following summer in
1878 they visited them at Naworth, where
May painted this watercolour. A note on
the reverse of this painting in May's hand
states that she presented it to her mother
as a gift. **RB**

33

Copy of a Renaissance drawing

May Morris, signed and inscribed

'21 Nov. 1879'

Pencil on paper

31.2 x 20.7 (12 $\frac{1}{4}$ x 8 $\frac{1}{8}$)

Mark Samuels Lasner Collection,

University of Delaware Library

This carefully observed pencil drawing of a young boy was possibly part of a class exercise at the National Art Training School, which May attended from October 1878. It appears to be copied from a Renaissance original and is an unusual departure from the landscape and architectural views that typify May's surviving watercolours and sketches. Students at the School were encouraged to make use of the collections in the neighbouring South Kensington Museum. **RB**

34

The Yard at Kelmscott

May Morris, inscribed 'Aug: 1878'

Pencil on paper

17.4 x 25 (6 $\frac{7}{8}$ x 9 $\frac{7}{8}$)

Ashmolean Museum (WA1941.108.12), 1941

This drawing is one of a set of eleven detailed architectural studies by May of the Kelmscott Manor estate. Probably preparatory studies for watercolours, they document the various buildings on the estate, from the Manor's attics and yard to the old barn, and are some of the earliest depictions of Kelmscott. May's handwritten observations on some of the studies reveal her acute attention to detail, noting distinctive architectural features such as mullioned windows, moulding around the chimneys and the play of shadows on the roof. **RB**

35

A street in Lyme Regis and the Cobb
in Lyme Regis, from a sketchbook of
landscapes and coastal scenes around
Bournemouth and Lyme Regis
May Morris, November 1882 – March 1883
Green cloth and morocco binding, pencil
drawings and watercolours
13.4 x 18.7 x 1.3 (5 $^1/_4$ x 7 $^3/_8$ x $^1/_2$)
V&A (E.209–1942) Given by Sir William
Rothenstein

During the winter of 1882–83, May, Jenny
and Jane Morris left London for the benefit
of Jenny's health, spending the winter in
the milder climate of the south coast of
England, first in Bournemouth before
moving to Lyme Regis where they had
relations, and where May enjoyed sketching
outdoors. This book, its pages watermarked
1881, and inscribed with her name on the
cover, is filled with watercolour and pencil
sketches of the area. A favourite spot
was the curved stone pier in Lyme Regis
harbour, known as the Cobb, which
features in several sketches in this book
and in a single watercolour probably also
painted during this visit.[11] **RB**

36

Kelmscott Manor and Merton Abbey, from
a sketchbook of views in Italy and England
May Morris, 1884–85
Pencil, watercolour, woven paper,
leather and cloth
18.9 x 26.1 x 1.4 (7 1/2 x 10 1/4 x 1/2)
V&A (E.210–1942) Given by Sir William
Rothenstein

This sketchbook contains views of
Kelmscott Manor, the river Thames near
the Morrises' house in Hammersmith
and also architectural studies of Genoa and
Turin where May travelled with her mother
in February 1885. It also contains one
of the earliest artistic impressions of the
Morris & Co. workshops at Merton Abbey.
The large building contained the tapestry,
carpet and block-printing workshops;
adjacent is the small washing shed. May
later recalled impressions of Merton Abbey
and how 'where the ramshackle, black-
boarded, red-tiled sheds were grouped
irregularly, all was life and activity'.[12] **RB**

37
The Drawing Room, Kelmscott House
May Morris, *c.* 1878–81
Pencil and watercolour on paper
22 x 25.4 (8 5/8 x 10)
WMG (D294iv) Purchased by Mr and Mrs
Harmer Brown at the Kelmscott Manor
sale July 1939

The Morris family moved to 26 Upper Mall (renaming it Kelmscott House) in 1878. May's detailed account of the house describes this elegant first-floor room with 'the discreet glimmer of old glass in closed cabinets sunk in the walls, and on a long narrow table lay a few pots and plates from the Far East'.[13] William Morris had an extensive collection of Middle Eastern carpets and textiles, which he displayed at Kelmscott House, such as the rug shown here covering the table. On the left a woman is playing a piano; this was later moved upstairs to Jane's bedroom. Both chairs depicted were produced by Morris & Co. **RB**

38

Bedroom at The Grange, Fulham

May Morris, early 1880s

Pencil and watercolour on paper

20 x 24 (7 $^{7}/_{8}$ x 9 $^{1}/_{2}$)

WMG (D294xi) Purchased by Mr and Mrs

Harmer Brown at the Kelmscott Manor

sale July 1939

The Grange was the family home of
Edward and Georgiana Burne-Jones.
Left unfinished, this intimate watercolour
illustrates their daughter Margaret's
bedroom. The cosy domestic scene shows
a drying rack in use and a dressing gown
hanging on the back of the door. The room
is furnished with a canopied bed and
book-lined shelves, with pictures on
the walls and, between the lustre vases
on the mantelshelf, two brass candlesticks
designed by Philip Webb, William Morris's
friend and collaborator. **RB**

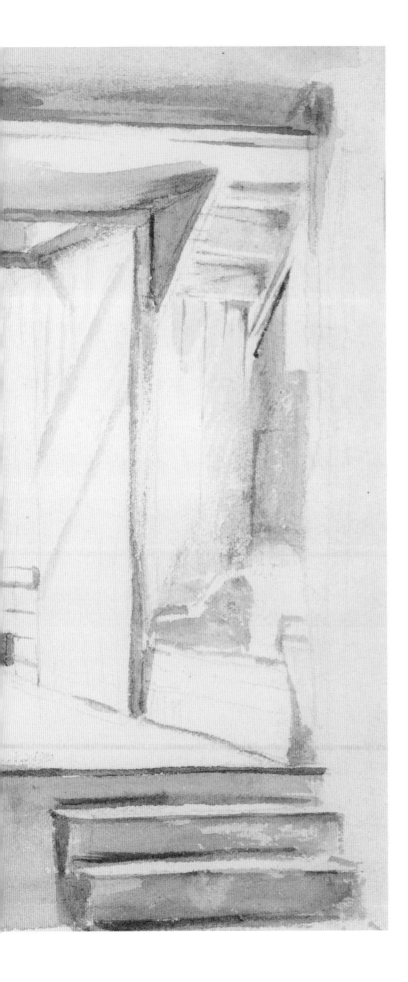

39

The Coach House, Kelmscott House

May Morris, *c.* 1878–81

Pencil and watercolour on paper

20 x 24 (7⅞ x 9½)

WMG (D294vii) Purchased by Mr and Mrs
Harmer Brown at the Kelmscott Manor
sale July 1939

William Morris began experimenting with
carpet production in the late 1870s, using
the adjoining former coach house of his
home in Hammersmith to accommodate
the carpet looms shown here. By 1881,
carpet production was moved to the
workshops at Merton Abbey, but not before
his hand-knotted carpets had become
known as 'Hammersmith' rugs and carpets.
The platform shown here served as a useful
stage soon after, when the coach house
was converted to become the meeting
place of the Hammersmith Branch of the
Socialist League (later the Hammersmith
Socialist Society). **RB**

40

Valentine card, 1886
May Morris
Pen and ink, watercolour and bodycolour
on paper on card
26.6 x 18.6 (10 $\frac{1}{2}$ x 7 $\frac{3}{8}$)
British Library, George Bernard Shaw
Papers (MS 50563, f.6 recto)

May made this Valentine for her friend the
Socialist and critic George Bernard Shaw;
it was discovered by chance in an album
of greeting cards. An inscription on the
verso in his hand confirms the date '14th
February 1886', and his diary notes: 'Got a
handsome Valentine.'[14] Knowing May to be
the artist, Shaw playfully informed her of
the gift, to which she replied: 'I must not
forget to ask you about this wonderful
Valentine. What female pen think you, was
bold enough to put down on paper the
inscrutable countenance of GBS?'[15] The
Valentine represents the height of May's
infatuation with Shaw, when the two were
often in each other's company, attending
concerts, plays and art exhibitions.

In the design the influences of
Pre-Raphaelitism and Aesthetic art are in
evidence through the fusing of a musical
subject with images of young women.
A procession of beautiful girls in long
flowing gowns, some bearing flowers as
votive offerings, comes to worship before
the sacred fire dedicated to Shaw. The
smoke from the flames bears aloft a
banner inscribed with a verse, above which
a scroll carries musical notation, crowned
by a portrait of Shaw.

As their friendship developed, May
became familiar with Shaw's personal
taste in art, which included the work of
Burne-Jones and J. M. Strudwick; his own
collection included a print of Burne-Jones's
The Golden Stairs (1880), in which May is
depicted. Officially appointed art critic of
the *World* in February 1886, Shaw was also
establishing his reputation as a music critic.
While May's inclusion on the Valentine of
the opening bars of love songs by Robert
Schumann (the composition to the left is
'Seit ich ihn gesehen') and Michel Lambert
(to the right is 'Il n'est point d'amour sans
peine') reveals her romantic sensibilities,
it was equally designed to appeal to
Shaw's musical interests, and reflected
their shared pleasure in performing music
together. Shaw's diaries recorded evenings
of 'playing and singing' with May, together
with Socialist League entertainments
where their duets took centre stage.[16]

Undoubtedly fond of May, Shaw was
in no position financially to extend his
friendship to matrimony. He would later
maintain that a 'Mystic Betrothal'[17] had
occurred between them, yet this did not
prevent him from establishing other close
relationships, and in 1885 he had begun an
affair with an older woman, Jenny Patterson.
May's verse pokes gentle fun at Shaw,
wittily alluding to the acerbic tones he
relied on as a critic ('your very crochets
form no bar'), and noting his philandering
with musical analogies: 'none can play
upon our hearts save you: within each breast
you strike a tender chord.' **ALICE MCEWAN**

Our time is yours; we care not for the rest
    Of your base sex: let each pursue his way,
    Its tenor moves us not; since none can play
Upon our hearts save you: within each breast
You strike a tender chord. Flatly confest,
    Minor considerations hold no sway
    We take our tone from you: be grave, be gay!
    Be sharp! be natural! we like it best!
Even your very crochets form no bar
    To our affection; just the minimum
Of kindness — one brief note! one little line
Is all we ask, the while we stand afar
And sing your praise in chorus, till she come
Who finds the key to your heart's inmost shrine.

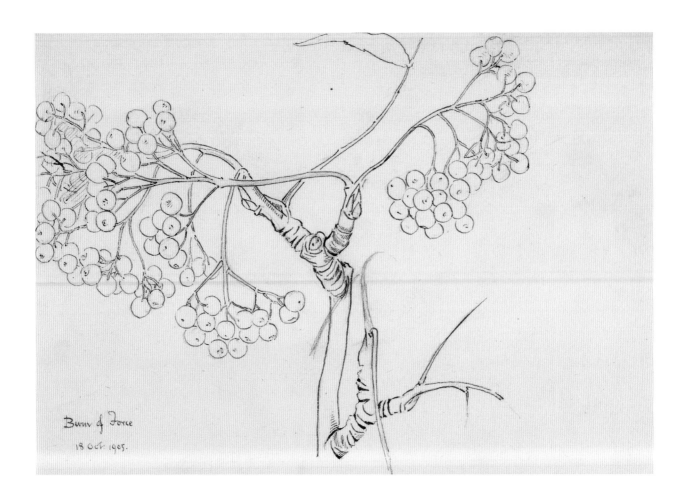

ABOVE

41

Burn of Force

May Morris, inscribed '18 Oct. 1905'

Ink and pencil on paper

17.5 x 25.5 (6 7/8 x 10)

Ashmolean Museum (OA1290)

OPPOSITE

42

Botanical studies

May Morris, probably October 1905

Pencil on paper

23.5 x 20.8 (9 1/4 x 8 1/8)

Ashmolean Museum (OA1293)

May had an excellent knowledge of flowers and plants and many of her surviving letters are filled with descriptions of the garden at Kelmscott Manor. Her illustration of a rowan branch at Burn of Force is one of a series drawn on a visit to Melsetter, the house owned by her friends the Middlemore family [see figs 94–96] on the remote island of Hoy, Orkney. Unlike her father, for whom no such observational botanical sketches survive, these drawings show May working directly from nature and were possibly executed as preparations for her embroidery designs. **RB**

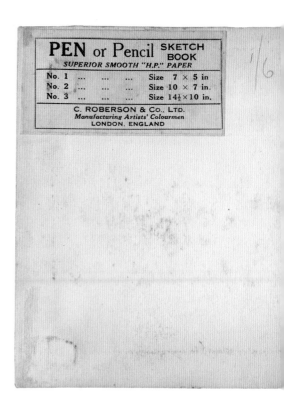

BELOW

43

Landscape with tent

May Morris, *c.* 1920–30

Watercolour on paper

17.8 x 25.7 (7 x 10⅛)

Mark Samuels Lasner Collection,

University of Delaware Library

May's watercolours from later life
continue to show her love of drawing out
of doors. Here her white bell tent is just
visible at the bottom of a deep valley in
north Wales. Encouraged by her
companion Mary Lobb, May proved an
enthusiastic camper and the pair went
on several camping trips around the
British Isles in the 1920s and 1930s.
A photograph of this same view is
in the National Library of Wales, part
of a collection of watercolours, photos
and ephemera donated by Lobb in 1939.

RB

ABOVE

44

Sketchbook; Views of Iceland

May Morris, *c.* 1924–29

Cloth, elastic band, pencil and ink on paper

13 x 18 (5 1/8 x 7)

The William Andrews Clark Memorial
Library, UCLA (MS.2010.009)

May followed in her father's footsteps,
visiting Iceland several times between
1924 and 1931. William Morris was
inspired to visit the country after reading
the Icelandic sagas, even learning the
language so he could translate them.
During May's visits to the country with
Mary Lobb, they travelled on horseback,
staying in local houses, including the
family home of Gudrun Jonsdottir, who
later recalled May painting 'the places
her father had described in his poems,
capturing them in watercolours to look
at in her home in Kelmscott Manor'.[18] **RB**

3

Wallpapers and Embroidery

ROWAN BAIN, JENNY LISTER, ANNA MASON

45
Fruit Garden portière or hanging
[detail of fig. 83]

EMBROIDERED TEXTILES WERE the first furnishings
designed and produced by William Morris. When Morris, Marshall,
Faulkner & Co. was established in 1861, friends and family helped
with the embroidery production, but as the business grew, it needed
specialist management, initially undertaken by May's mother, Jane
Morris, and Jane's sister, Elizabeth Burden, who were both talented
embroiderers. Their tasks included overseeing outworkers, providing
materials and patterns, paying wages and keeping accounts.

With her mother and aunt as role models, May became the manager
of the Morris & Co. embroidery department in 1885, at the age of 23.
She was ideally suited to this position, having shown artistic aptitude
from a young age, and she had been provided with a unique creative
education. Her mother taught her to embroider, and her father shared
his appreciation and knowledge of many different crafts and, crucially,
involved her in his design work. Having studied at the National
Art Training School,[1] by the mid-1880s May was an accomplished
embroiderer and designer, and it was natural that she would become
involved with the family business. To begin with this was an informal
arrangement, and May produced some wallpaper designs before taking
over the embroidery department.

By this time Morris & Co. had a very effective business model, with
a trademark style notable for the use of natural dyes and the quality of
stitching and design. A great variety of embroidered items was displayed
at the Oxford Street showroom: room and fire screens, portières and
wall hangings, cushions, bags, chair covers, mats and tablecloths.
Customers could choose a kit (that included threads, the design drawn
onto the fabric and a stitched area for guidance), or a finished object.
There were items to suit all budgets, with a completed portière at £47
and a kit of the same design for £3. Bespoke options were also offered,

OPPOSITE
46
Pomona hanging
Designed by Edward Burne-Jones
and William Morris
Executed by three embroiderers
at the Royal School of
Needlework, arranged and
worked under the direction of
May Morris and Miss Barker,
1891
Silk on linen
Stitches include long and short
stitches, and laid and couched
work
Embroidered motto 'I am the
ancient apple-queen · as once
I was so am I now · for evermore
a hope unseen · betwixt the
blossom and the bough · ah,
where's the river's hidden gold
· and where the windy grave of
troy yet come I as I came of old ·
from out the heart of summer's
joy', from William Morris, *Poems
by the Way* (1891)
297.2 x 213.4 (117 x 84)
Private collection

i am the ancient apple-queen · as once i was · so am i now.
for evermore a hope unseen · betwixt the blossom and the bough ·

ahwheres the rivers hidden gold · and where the windy grave of troy
yet come i as i came of old · from out the heart of summers ioy ·

where patrons chose a different colour scheme or background fabric, had an existing design adapted, or a new embroidery designed. May was creatively restricted in her design choices, however, in having to adhere to the strong Morris & Co. brand. Resulting uncertainties in attribution led to the underestimation of May's importance to the business, then as well as now. In 1893, for example, one newspaper printed a correction to its review of the Arts and Crafts exhibition, which had mistakenly attributed a bed hanging [fig. 87], stating: 'Miss May Morris is very anxious to disclaim for her father the designing and colouring of a very interesting piece of wool-work on linen, which she says is not from his hand, but her own, and she thinks that those who know Mr William Morris's style of design ought not have made this mistake', before adding: 'Nevertheless, the specimen of such hangings "from a bed in Kelmscott Manor, Lechlade" is excellent enough for the lady who made the design to be proud of it, though she may modestly wish to disclaim any praise which naturally belongs to her father's own manner of work.'[2]

May inherited some outworkers in 1885, but additional embroiderers were needed as the workload increased. She began by recruiting acquaintances such as Lily Yeats (sister to the poet W. B. Yeats) for the workroom then based at Kelmscott House, the Morris home. When more staff were required, May leased premises at Iffley Road, Hammersmith, employing the actress Florence Farr, the Irish language activist Norma Borthwick and Euphrosyne Pappajannopoulo (known as Mrs Stefan), of London's Greek community. For an apprentice, she enquired at the local board school for a girl who showed promise. Fourteen-year-old Ellen Wright was chosen.[3]

Overall the staff were fortunate in their working conditions, in stark contrast to others working in the notoriously exploitative textile industry, where, as one contemporary put it, they were paid not a living wage but a 'lingering, dying wage'.[4] Ellen Wright began on an apprentice wage of four shillings a week. All staff had incremental rises as their skills progressed, and Lily Yeats's wage rose from seventeen to thirty shillings a week in the period 1888–94. Unlike the twelve-hour day of less fortunate textile workers, the hours were also reasonable, at 10 a.m.–6 p.m. Monday to Friday, and a half day on Saturday. These conditions were comparable to those for staff at the Royal School of Art Needlework; this was an organization the Morris family knew well, with William Morris providing designs for their embroiderers and May's aunt, Elizabeth Burden, teaching there.

May provided tuition to her employees, because although her older staff were competent needlewomen, they needed to be trained in the Morris embroidery style. As Lily Yeats became more experienced, she assisted with this training and supervision, especially of the apprentices. May remained in charge of pricing, liaison with clients, design, ensuring enough stock was available for the shop, fulfilling orders and the quality of the final product. As well as embroidery, one of the main tasks that the department undertook was transferring design outlines onto fabric. Morris & Co. preferred to use the traditional method, rather than using pre-printed embroidery designs. A paper design was pricked with a needle and charcoal rubbed over or pounced through the holes onto the ground, providing a guide to enable the design outline to be painted or inked on the fabric, ready for embroidering. This was a skilled job, and one that customers were pleased to pay for.

In 1890, May married and moved the department to her new home at 8 Hammersmith Terrace, London. By this time, only Lily Yeats and Ellen Wright remained, and May recruited a second apprentice, Maud Deacon. The Morris & Co. Embroidery Day Book [fig. 51] shows that from 1892 to 1896 there were 453 orders for a total of 670 items, almost all for designs drawn on fabric, which meant the small number of staff could manage this quantity of work. Although only 1.5 per cent of the orders were for finished embroideries, these accounted for half the total income. Altogether the department invoiced customers for £1,186 over those four years, equivalent to about £70,000 today.[5] This was a modest contribution to the company as a whole, though, because Morris & Co. could realize estimated profits of nearly £10,000 a year (as achieved in 1891).[6]

May was an extremely effective manager and supervisor, and her abilities were sought after by other organizations; for example, she oversaw production of the magnificent *Pomona* [fig. 46] at the Royal School of Art Needlework.[7] Yet overall it was her ability to design that was crucial to her success at Morris & Co. This is where May differed from her predecessors at the company (including her mother and her aunt). Her designs were so accomplished because she had a deep knowledge of embroidery technique, combined with artistic ability and training.

May left the department in 1896, the year her father died, having managed it for eleven years. She went on to pursue her varied interests, including teaching, writing, editing and private embroidery projects, away from the restrictions of designing in the Morris style and product range.

The following pages illustrate surviving examples of May's designs for Morris & Co., which include wallpapers as well as embroideries, retailed from the 1880s (pp. 62–117). Her work also included stitched panels designed earlier by William Morris. The sequence traces the development of May's style, extending and adapting the Morris & Co. vocabulary of patterns and motifs for embroidery. The subsequent pages (pp. 118–51) represent her independent work and personal commissions from about 1890 until the 1930s, the last decade of her life.

CATHERINE WHITE

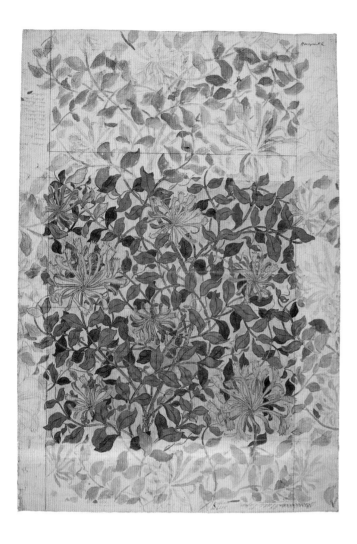

47

Design for *Honeysuckle*

May Morris, *c.* 1883

Pencil and watercolour on paper

99.6 x 68.6 (39 1/4 x 27)

William Morris Society (C7) Bequeathed

by Helena Stephenson, 1970

OPPOSITE

48

Honeysuckle

Designed by May Morris, manufactured

by Jeffrey & Co. for Morris & Co., *c.* 1883

Blockprinted in distemper colour

Width 55.9 (22), pattern repeat 54 (21 1/4)

WMG (B52)

In the early days of her involvement with Morris & Co., May designed three wallpapers. *Honeysuckle* was her most popular and enduring pattern, its light and uplifting design proving very successful for the firm. Based on a net structure of untamed woody stems, small curling leaves in two tones and honeysuckle flowers set against a plain background, the design was produced in four colourways.

Debate surrounds who originally designed *Honeysuckle*, some arguing that William Morris was in fact responsible. This is based on its earliest known attribution from 1890 crediting it to William Morris.[8] However, it was not unusual for designs by both May and John Henry Dearle, Morris & Co.'s chief designer, to be credited to the firm's more famous owner in order to make the products more commercially viable. The first time the design was attributed to May is in the Morris & Co. wallpaper catalogue from about 1912.

The original design, now in the collection of the William Morris Society, provides few clues to clarify the attribution. The paper is watermarked 'J Whatman 1879' and shows soft pencil outlines filled with watercolour. Annotated instructions reveal eight woodblocks were required to achieve the finished pattern, which was numbered 6575. On the reverse is written 'Mr. Morris Esq' and the address of Merton Abbey. The design is heavily worked over in parts, suggesting that May was the main designer, but as a novice she perhaps sought help from her father to complete it.

Although May was no longer involved with the company by 1912, given her role in fortifying William Morris's legacy it is unlikely that she would have tolerated a public misattribution if indeed her father were the designer. Moreover, *Honeysuckle* is notably absent from *William Morris: Artist, Writer, Socialist* in which May listed her father's forty most successful wallpaper designs,[9] which adds further weight to the argument identifying May as the designer. **RB**

49

Horn Poppy

Designed by May Morris, manufactured by Jeffrey & Co. for Morris & Co., *c.* 1885

Blockprinted in distemper colour

Width 56.3 (22 1/8), pattern repeat 51 (20)

WMG (B155) Given by Peter Jamieson, 2013

The horned poppy was one of May's favourite floral motifs, frequently incorporated into her designs for embroidery. In 1885, she used the flower for this wallpaper design, setting the meandering stems with open and closed flowers against a pin-dotted background; a device used in other Morris & Co. wallpaper patterns issued around this time, including *Pink and Poppy*, *Wild Tulip* and *Grafton*. The firm printed *Horn Poppy* in ten colourways and the swirling design proved so popular with customers that it was in continuous production from the start. **RB**

50

Arcadia

Designed by May Morris, manufactured by Jeffrey & Co. for Morris & Co., *c.* 1886

Blockprinted in distemper colour

Width 53.3 (21), pattern repeat 68 (26 3/4)

V&A (E.555–1919) Given by Morris and Co.

Despite the popularity of May's designs, *Arcadia*, created in 1886, was her final wallpaper design for the firm. From 1886 to 1896, she seems to have worked exclusively on embroidery. The design for *Arcadia* incorporates twisting floral stems set against a background of smaller foliage and tiny flowers. Morris & Co.'s wallpaper pattern book from around 1915 shows they produced the pattern in four different colourways including blue, brown and red. The holes derive from use in the pattern book. **RB**

51

Morris & Co. Embroidery Day Book
Handwritten ledger by May Morris
May 1892 – November 1896
Marbled paper covered board with
leather binding
32.3 x 21.4 x 2.7 (12 $^3/_4$ x 8 $^1/_2$ x 1 $^1/_8$) (closed)
V&A National Art Library
(MSL/1939/2636) Bequeathed by
May Morris

The Day Book contains detailed evidence of the work of the Morris & Co. embroidery business under May's management. It records 453 numbered orders, together with the client's name, a design name and the item to be embroidered. May also specified the ground fabric, usually 'M. clo' for 'Manchester cloth', or a Morris & Co. silk, with a reference number, the type of thread required, whether or not a 'started' kit, and its price. Usually, she added the date the order was completed. About 40 per cent of orders were supplied as stock or samples for the shop; square panels and cushion covers were the most popular, representing 37 per cent of the 670 items ordered.

The range and quantity of the ninety-two named designs demonstrate the longevity of some 1870s designs by William Morris [see figs 52, 55 and 58] and the commercial appeal of May's new designs. For example, *Tulip*, a table cover shown at the 1890 Arts and Crafts exhibition, was ordered thirty-two times. The workroom manufactured finished products from a *Rose* pincushion charged at 3s. 6d., to the four *Fruit Garden* hangings for Mrs J. (Mary) Monro Longyear, costing a total of £182, the most expensive order in the book [figs 74–76].

The Day Book lists 153 customers, including established clients such as Mrs Ionides, Mrs Barr Smith and Mrs Middlemore, some of whose purchases are now in museum collections [see figs 69, 70 and 83]. One notable order came from the Chicago department store Marshall Field's in July 1895, for a large tablecloth worked on '19/1400' silk with filoselle and twist, specially designed but with the embroidery just started, for completion presumably in Chicago, for £20. Titled clients with ancestral homes to furnish included Lady Hindlip, Lady Trevelyan and the Countess of Rosslyn, but most customers and their addresses are frustratingly untraceable. However, the number of clients indicates the accessibility of the Morris & Co. range for amateur embroiderers. Ephemeral correspondence at the back of the Day Book, some relating to the Kelmscott hangings [fig. 87], reveal further details of accounting for workroom time. Only six orders for church furnishings are recorded, including three altar frontals.

While the 1892–96 Day Book is the only existing record of the daily transactions of the embroidery workroom from her eleven years in charge, May ensured it survived to illustrate the success of her management, as it was bequeathed by her to the V&A.[10] With the embroideries and the archive of designs and tracings at the Museum, it reveals a determination to preserve her own legacy, as well as that of her father. JL

November 1892

95. 0. 0	No 1363 Mrs J. Monro Longyear May 30th 92 2 "Fruit Garden" Portières, Damask, Silk 8' 8" × 4. 6"		Apl. 25th 93
87. 0. 0	No 1364 Mrs J. Monro Longyear May 30th 92 2 8'. 8" × 3		June 28th 93
18. 0. 0	No 1340 Henderson Esq. May 31st 92 Altar Frontal & Super Frontal, Red damask silk for altar 2. 9" high × 5. 6" long		Jan 1st 1894
- 17. 0	No 1354 Mrs Barr Smith May 28th 92 1 Cushion 2½" × 3½" M. clo. (Fuschia) Jan. 31. 93		
1. 5 0	No 1356 Mrs Barr Smith May 28th Work Bag . Silk Jany. 27th 93		
0 10. 6 0 12. 0	No 1357-8 Mrs Barr Smith May 28th 2 Bands for Work Bag - M clo:		
£1. 5. 0	No 1411 Mrs Barr Smith Aug 19th Decr 3 Mantle Border - M clo:		
1. 4. 0	No 1445 Stock Nov. 3rd Dec. 13 2 Autumn Cushions - M clo.		
0. 17. 0	No 1447 Stock Nov 3rd 29 Nov 2 Myrtle Leaf Panels - M clo.		
0. 11. 0	No 1448 Stock Nov 3rd Feb 13th 2 Small Tulips Panels - M clo.		

52 and 53
Acanthus bedcover or hanging
Designed by William Morris, *c.* 1880
Worked by May Morris and others,
c. 1900–1910 (probably)
Coloured silk thread on woollen felt cloth,
edged with silk cord
Worked in darning stitch, long and short
stitch, stem stitch, satin stitch, buttonhole
stitch, couching and laid work
248.8 x 200.6 (98 x 79)
V&A (T.66–1939) Bequeathed by May
Morris

Acanthus was one of William Morris's
most popular compositions, reproduced
for many years after it was first designed.
Its quartered configuration reflects Morris's
preoccupation with hand-knotted carpets
from the late 1870s. When shown on a

bed, the embroidered panel would have
been removed each night by a housemaid
and folded up on a chair. At the time these
embroideries, which covered only the top
of the bed, were also known as quilts or
cot quilts, although they were not made
with wadding and quilting stitches. It was
suitable for use both as a bedcover and
a decorative hanging.

The completed design looks dramatically
different depending on stitches, colours
and amount of ground remaining as part
of the final effect. This example from May's
own collection is one of three *Acanthus*
embroideries at the V&A, and is a highly
original later interpretation exhibited in
Paris in 1914.[11] Its coloured silks on a
bright blue wool ground contrasts with
two versions worked soon after Morris
produced the design in about 1880: a large
hanging worked in muted tones of wool
on pale linen, made by Florence Bell and

her daughters for Rounton Grange,
Northallerton (Circ.524–1953), and
a smaller sample hanging probably
shown at the Morris & Co. shop
worked with silk entirely covering
the cotton ground (T.153–1979).

May recorded twenty-eight orders
for *Acanthus* (including some small
versions) in the Day Book, although
only one is described as a quilt.
Most are for panels on Manchester
cloth, although further analysis is
complicated by the fact that various
versions of *Acanthus* were available.[12]

A working drawing is in the V&A
(E.55–1940). JL

54

Flowerpot design

William Morris, *c.* 1876

Pencil and ink on paper

58.5 x 59.1 (23 x 23 ¹/₄)

WMG (A1061) Given by Arthur Todd, 2002

55

Flowerpot panel

Embroidered by May Morris,

c. mid-1880s–90s

Coloured silks and gold thread on linen

Worked in stem stitch, satin stitch, darning stitch, herringbone, French knot and couching

52.1 x 52.1 (20 ¹/₂ x 20 ¹/₂)

WMG (F154) Given by Marie Lyndon Lang, 1954

These two embroidered panels [figs 55, 56] illustrate the skill and creativity with which May interpreted her father's designs. *Flowerpot* was one of Morris's last designs for embroidery and was inspired by two panels of seventeenth-century French or Italian lacis work acquired by the South Kensington Museum in 1875.[13] The William Morris Gallery's design is watermarked 1876. *Flowerpot* was popular for cushion covers and fire screens and could be purchased as a finished embroidery or in kit form.[14]

At the 1890 Arts and Crafts exhibition May displayed a version described as a cushion and she showed a framed screen in New York in 1910.[15] The embroideries seen here were worked by May herself. Fig. 55 was gifted by May to her friend Dorothy Walker, daughter of the printer Emery Walker. May loaned fig. 56 to the V&A's William Morris centenary exhibition in 1934 and later bequeathed it to the Museum.[16] Other worked examples are in the collections of National Museums Liverpool,

Birmingham Museum and Art Gallery and the Embroiderers' Guild.

These two examples demonstrate the freedom and variety of May's interpretation. Fig. 55 is worked in silks and couched Japanese gold thread. Using a small vocabulary of stitches – stem, satin, herringbone and French knots – May expertly juxtaposes different textures. A small area of darning stitch is used to 'fill in' the green stems, rising out of the vase, but the majority of the motifs are worked in outline only. The panel is edged in handmade yellow silk buttonhole braid.

Fig. 56, worked on a felted wool, demonstrates the potential offered by combining alternative grounds, coloured threads and stitches. May achieved a more delicate effect with this version, using pastel shades of silk worked almost entirely in chain stitch, and just a few outlines and motifs worked in satin and stem stitch. Tiny dispersed running stitches, or 'speckling', worked on the flowers in the same colour as the ground, add dots of light to the dense cream wool. **AM & JL**

56

Flowerpot panel

Embroidered by May Morris, 1890–1900

Coloured silks on wool

Worked in chain stitch, satin stitch,

stem stitch and speckling

54.6 x 54.6 (21¹/₂ x 21¹/₂)

V&A (T.68–1939) Bequeathed by May Morris

57

Olive and Rose embroidery kit (started)

Designed by William Morris, *c.* 1880;
probably retailed *c.* 1900

Coloured silks and ink on cotton

Worked in darning stitch

64.5 x 68.6 (25 x 27)

V&A (Circ.300–1960) Given by Miss Vere Roberts

58

Olive and Rose fire screen

Designed by William Morris, *c.* 1880

Coloured silks on silk, mahogany frame

Worked in stem stitch, satin stitch and darning stitch

56.5 x 57.6 (22 1/4 x 22 5/8) (embroidered panel)

119 x 64 x 32 (46 7/8 x 25 1/8 x 12 5/8) (frame)

Fire screen stamped with MORRIS & CO / (4)49 OXFORD ST W / 1221

Private collection

Olive and Rose was one of William Morris's most popular embroidered panels and it was still available over thirty years after it had been designed, in *c.* 1912, when the *Embroidery Work* catalogue was printed. It is illustrated as a panel and a fire screen, priced at £4. 10s., a fee that included 'stretching and mounting customers' own embroidery under glass'.[17]

The design was ordered thirteen times between 1892 and 1896, when, according to the Day Book, ten cushion kits were supplied as stock for the Oxford Street shop. The uncompleted kit in the V&A collection was intended to be stitched with pale yellow flowers, dark red olives and deep green stems, against an olive green ground completely filled with darning stitches.

The completed example, with a restrained palette of pale pinks and cool greens, has dark outlines meticulously worked in stem stitch, filled with darning stitch. Distinctive satin-stitched rose thorns stand out sharply against the cream silk ground. Given the quality of the stitching, it was probably worked in the embroidery department at Morris & Co.

Other versions are in the collections of the Whitworth Gallery, Manchester, and Wallington, Northumberland (National Trust). A fire screen with an *Olive and Rose* panel embroidered by Mrs Hodson of Compton Hall was sold in 2013.[18] JL

59
Rose Wreath panel
Designed by William Morris
Embroidered by May Morris, *c.* 1890
Coloured silks on linen
Worked in darning stitch, satin stitch
and long and short stitch
51 x 51 (20 x 20)
WMG (F435) Given by Diana
Hillman, 2014

Rose Wreath was exhibited at the Arts and Crafts exhibition in 1890. The design by William Morris of a central rose bush surrounded by a wreath of oak leaves was embroidered by May as a cushion cover. This example was a present from May to her friend Amy Carruthers Tozer (1867–1961), daughter of John Carruthers, William Morris's friend and fellow member of the Hammersmith Socialist Society. Further examples of the design include a cushion worked by American heiress Annie May Hegeman, now in the Cooper Hewitt, Smithsonian Design Museum, New York (1941.71.1). **RB**

60

Tudor Rose panel

Designed by May Morris, *c.* 1890

Embroidered by Alice Mary Godman

Coloured silks on linen

Worked in darning stitch, stem stitch
and long and short stitch

67.3 x 67.3 (26 1/2 x 26 1/2)

Rhode Island School of Design Museum
(85.200 Farago Art Fund)

The *Tudor Rose* design, with a centred motif filling the whole screen, shows an alternative to the square panels designed around a plant growing from the base such as *Rose Wreath* [fig. 59]. The Day Book records one order for the design, a kit on gold '14/1400' silk for a Mrs Wiggins.[19] A traced design is in the V&A Archive of Art and Design, and the V&A was given another incomplete version in 1976.[20] This panel was worked by Dame Alice Godman (1868–1944), Deputy President of the British Red Cross Society. JL

Maids of Honour design

Designed by May Morris, *c.* 1880–92

Red ink on paper, pounced for transfer

55.3 x 30.5 (21 3/4 x 12)

V&A (E.956–1954) Bequeathed by
May Morris

'Welcome maids of honour. You do bring in the spring and wait upon her' is the opening of 'To Violets' by the seventeenth-century poet Robert Herrick. In this design, May illustrates the violets and damask roses featured in the poem to create one of her most harmonious and attractive embroidery designs. The central rose bush is surrounded by a ring of violets, with a bird in flight in each corner. The subtle colour palette of white, purple, pale green and orange is expertly shaded, using long and short stitch to achieve a soft and elegant effect [figs 62, 63].

Also referred to as 'Birds and Violets', the design is frequently recorded in the Day Book for both screens and cushions; it cost 13 shillings. Two pricked tracings in the V&A, and embroidered examples in the William Morris Gallery, Manchester Metropolitan University Special Collections, the Art Gallery of South Australia and other private collections, confirm it was a commercial success for the firm.

Fig. 63 was worked by May herself and is embroidered on a very fine silk mesh called a silk canvas (also known as Berlin canvas). This expensive backing demanded great skill and precision owing to the transparent quality that made threads at the back more visible. Mounted on a wooden stretcher, the canvas was then framed, some being set into fire screens, like that belonging to the Barr Smith family now in the Art Gallery of South Australia (977A66). Unusually, May departed from her own advice in *Decorative Needlework*, where she suggests lightly shaded petals should be treated 'with a firm outline to render the pattern clear'.[21] Here [fig. 63] the fine net background is left exposed to form a light outline around the petals. Any suggestion that this example was unfinished is contested by the same execution in the Manchester Metropolitan University version, also embroidered by May and sold by her to the School of Art there for £10 in 1909.

May exhibited the design many times, including at the 1906 Arts and Crafts exhibition; at the New Zealand International Exhibition in the same year where the execution was credited to both May and Maude Deacon, an employee at Morris & Co.; and in New York in 1910, during her American lecture tour. The version now in the William Morris Gallery [fig. 63] was kept by May and is possibly the same panel exhibited at the 1932 Society of Women Artists' annual exhibition in London. The panel was then purchased by Edward and Stephani Scott-Snell (later Godwin) at the Kelmscott Manor sale in 1939 and features in the background of a 1944 painting by Stephani or Edward in the dining room at Kelmscott where they were tenants.[22] **RB**

62

Maids of Honour panel

Designed and embroidered by

May Morris, *c.* 1890

Coloured silks on silk

Worked in satin, split, long and short stitch

57 x 55 (22 $^1/_2$ x 21 $^5/_8$)

Society of Antiquaries of London:

Kelmscott Manor (KM213) Given by

Frances Stillman, previously owned by

Marie Spartali Stillman

63
Maids of Honour panel
Designed and embroidered by
May Morris, *c.* 1890s
Coloured silks on silk net
Worked in satin, split, long and
short stitch
60 x 60 (23 5/8 x 23 5/8)
WMG (F368) Given by Stephani
Scott-Snell/Godwin, 1995

64

Embroidery design

May Morris, *c.* 1885

Pencil and Indian ink on calico

107.9 x 58.4 (42 ¹/₂ x 23)

V&A (E.959–1954) Bequeathed by

May Morris

This design or pattern for tracing directly onto glazed calico was probably drawn when May was developing her own style. The large tulips, roses and peonies, entwined with acanthus leaves, were a favourite choice for her father's designs, whereas smaller, countryside flowers were characteristic of May's later design vocabulary. The trellis framework was a structure May would return to for her later designs for the Kelmscott bed hangings [fig. 87]; there is also a *Trellis* design for a cushion panel recorded in the Day Book. JL

65

Westward Ho! design

May Morris, possibly early 1880s

Pencil, sepia and watercolour on paper

52.3 x 102.5 (20⅝ x 40⅜)

William Morris Society (D022)

Bequeathed by Helena Stephenson, 1970

66

Westward Ho! panel

Designed by May Morris

Embroidered by Jane Morris, possibly early 1880s

Coloured silks on unbleached linen

48.5 x 91 (19⅛ x 35⅞)

Worked in darning and satin stitch

William Morris Society (T004) Donated by Martin Fisher, 2008

Scrolling acanthus leaves and stylized poppies are enclosed within a chequered border. The design was named after the village on the North Devon coast, home to the United Services College where Cormell Price, a close family friend, was headmaster from 1874. The embroidery has an unidentified exhibition label inscribed in May's hand: 'Oblong mat: darning. Designed by May Morris. Worked by Mrs William Morris. Not for sale'. Four versions ordered in 1893 are listed in the Day Book. This embroidery remained with the Morris family and corresponds to an item listed in the Kelmscott Manor sale catalogue.[23] **AM**

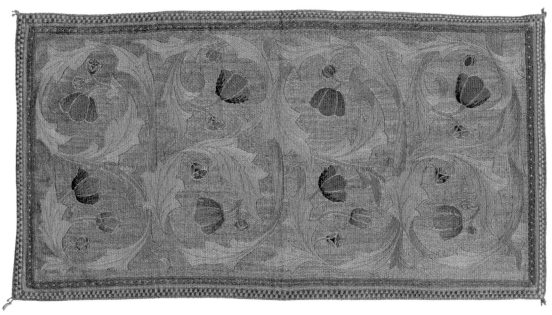

67

Design for 'embroidered panel
for a screen'
Signed 'MM'
Printed proof on paper
Illustrated in 'Chain-stitch embroidery',
Hobby Horse, 3, 1888, p. 24
9 x 7 (3 $1/2$ x 2 $3/4$)
WMG (K736) Given by the V&A from
the gift of Dr Robert Steele, 1955

This illustration accompanied May's first
article on embroidery, published when
she had been running the Morris & Co.
workroom for three years. The design, in
the Morris & Co. style, with twisting stems
around a central rose tree, and small,
attenuated tulips against a vermicelli
background, was later worked as a screen
panel in darning and stem stitch [see fig.
68], although originally May presumably
worked the design in chain stitch to use
it to illustrate her discussion of the merits
of the technique.

In the article May argues for the 'utility
of referring to good examples of old work
for instruction in this or any embroidery
stitch'[24] and suggests ways of achieving
'dainty effects' with outline work of small
chain stitches, which she greatly admired,
although the technique had declined
among hand embroiderers because of the
ease with which the sewing machine could
replicate it. Elsewhere she wrote: 'Some
of the most famous work in the world has
been wrought in this stitch, and many
important pieces remain to show us what
can be done in the way of minute and
laborious work combined with good
design and beautiful colour.'[25] Some of
May's surviving work illustrates this [see
fig. 56]. In this issue of *Hobby Horse* May
also advertised embroidery lessons. JL

68

Three-fold screen
Designed by J. H. Dearle and May Morris,
c. 1888
Mahogany frame with ebony banding,
glazed panels, with central drop leaf shelf,
embroidered with coloured silks on silk,
stitches include darning and stem stitch
Frame stamped twice 'Morris & Co 449
Oxford St West, numbered 1586'
177.3 x 51.3 (69 $3/4$ x 20 $1/4$) (side panels)
177.3 x 58.7 (69 $3/4$ x 23 $1/8$) (central panel)
Sold at Christie's, King Street, London,
3 November 1999, current location
unknown

69

Australia table cover
Designed by May Morris, *c*. 1888
Embroidered by Mary Barr Smith
Silk embroidery on silk with silk fringe
Stitches include darning and stem stitch
94 × 91 (37 × 35 3/4)
Art Gallery of South Australia (991A1)

Robert and Joanna Barr Smith were both born in Scotland and became extremely wealthy owing to highly profitable business interests in South Australia, including mining, farming and shipping. They lived in Adelaide, but made long visits to Britain. During the 1880s and 1890s they were among Morris & Co.'s most extravagant international clients, commissioning interior schemes for their two main homes, Torrens Park in Adelaide, and their summer house Auchendarroch, Mount Barker, in the Adelaide Hills. Both houses, and others owned by the following two generations of the family, were lavishly furnished with Morris & Co. wallpapers, furniture, carpets, tapestries, printed and woven textiles, and embroideries. The Barr Smith collection of furnishings now at the Art Gallery of South Australia is an outstanding record of the taste of these most enthusiastic Morris & Co. customers.

Joanna Barr Smith and her daughters and daughters-in-law were all keen embroiderers, who purchased many kits from the company including large portières such as *Acanthus*, a *Pigeon* hanging, and *Pomegranate*, *Vine* and *Apple Tree* screen panels. They also commissioned two new designs, including *Adelaide* and *Australia*, here worked by Mary Barr Smith (1863–1941), the wife of Robert and Joanna's son Tom. There are tracings and working drawings for both in the V&A Archive of Art and Design. Perhaps surprisingly, the *Australia* pattern, with large flowering stylized rose trees and tulips, does not incorporate Australian plants.[26] From 1892 to 1896 Joanna Barr Smith ordered fifteen kits, including the *Fruit Garden* portière worked by her daughter Erlistoun Mitchell (1868–1913), a work bag, nightdress case, a mantle border, and the *Gladiolus* table cover possibly seen in fig. 71, bought for 18 shillings. The family seem to have especially admired the tablecloths designed by May. Other designs stitched by Erlistoun Mitchell include a version of the spectacular *Vine Leaf* [fig. 97] and simpler examples such as *Poppy* [fig. 70] with narrower floral borders, often edging a dark green silk or velvet centre finished with a colour-matched fringe. As a tablecloth border, a *Poppy* kit cost 14s. 9d.[27] JL

70

Poppy table cover

Designed by May Morris, 1894 or before

Embroidered by Erlistoun Mitchell

Silk embroidery on linen, silk fringe

Stitches include darning and stem stitch

107 x 107 (42 ^{1}/$_8$ x 42 ^{1}/$_8$)

Art Gallery of South Australia (881A1A)

Gift of Joanna Simpson, 1988

71

Robert and Joanna Barr Smith in

the drawing room of Auchendarroch,

Mount Barker, Adelaide Hills, *c.* 1897

Ernest Gall

Photograph

State Library of South Australia, Adelaide

(PRG 354/50)

72

Rose Bush embroidery kit (started)

Designed by May Morris, *c.* 1890;

probably sold *c.* 1900

Coloured silks and ink on cotton

Worked in stem stitch and darning stitch

62.6 x 66 (24 5/8 x 26)

V&A (Circ.301–1960) Given by

Miss Vere Roberts

ABOVE

73

Rose Bush pattern used for tracing, *c.* 1900

Ink on glazed cotton

38.1 x 49.5 (15 x 19 1/2)

V&A (AAD/190/6 file 1) Bequeathed by

May Morris, 1939[28]

Often requested as a pair of cushion kits, *Rose Bush* appears ten times in the Day Book, mostly ordered as stock for the Morris & Co. shop. A design on paper is in the collection of the William Morris Society.[29] The design, with a large pair of Morris acanthus leaves combined with stylized rose sprays, uses a similar structure to *Olive and Rose* [figs 57, 58]. Once worked, with green stems and leaves, these would contrast with the bright blue silk darning-stitch ground.

The pattern drawn onto glazed cotton helps to demonstrate the kit production process, being used as a template from which the workroom staff made a tracing on paper for laying over the kit ground. The outlines were pricked through with a needle and charcoal dust rubbed or pounced through to leave fine dots on the fabric, which were then joined up with ink to produce the marked-up cloth, ready for embroidering. JL

74 and 75

Fruit Garden portière or hanging

(one of a pair)

Designed by May Morris, before 1890

Signed 'MM' lower left corner

Worked by May Morris and assistants

(probably), 1892–93

Silk damask, embroidered with silk, with

silk fringe and cotton lining

Worked in stem stitch, darning stitch,

satin stitch, herringbone stitch, buttonhole

stitch and pistil stitch with couching

Embroidered motto: 'All wrought by the

worm in the peasant carle's cot/On the

mulberry leafage when summer was hot'

257.8 x 137.2 (101 ¹/₂ x 54) (including fringe)

Museum of Fine Arts, Boston (1983.160c)

Given in memory of J. S. and Sayde Z.

Gordon from Myron K. and Natalie G. Stone

The *Fruit Garden* or *Fruit Tree*[30] portières have long been recognized as outstanding examples of art embroidery and show May Morris reaching the height of her abilities. The design combines sinuous young trees and swirling acanthus, united with an embroidered text. 'The Flowering Orchard', subtitled 'Silk embroidery', was written by William Morris for the purpose and published in *Poems by the Way* in 1891. The tree in the centre is surrounded by an orchard of trees bearing plums, pomegranates, apples and cherry blossoms, described by George Bernard Shaw as 'glowing fruit forests'.[31] The trees and plants are worked in simple stem and darning stitches, with some additional texture added in herringbone stitch, while the fruit and flowers are achieved with laid work, buttonhole stitches and pistil stitches creating extra detail. The rich effect of the silks is increased by the use of Morris & Co. 'Oak Leaf' damask, recommended by May.[32]

A *Fruit Garden* hanging embroidered on blue linen was one of nine embroideries exhibited by May at the 1890 Arts and Crafts exhibition. Several versions were commissioned, and the evidence of surviving examples and photographs show that they all had subtle differences, depending on size and the type of ground

fabric used. Four separate orders are recorded in the Day Book from 1892 to 1896.

The example illustrated here, the only known signed version, was ordered as a pair by Mary Monro Longyear of Marquette, Michigan, on 30 May 1892, together with another narrower pair [see fig. 76] with a complementary but different design. Both sets were worked by May, presumably with assistants helping on the unsigned panels, and completed by 28 June 1893. Each pair cost £95 and £87 respectively. The inscriptions on the second pair are from the thirteenth-century English round 'Summer is icumen in', while its inspiration is drawn from medieval *opus anglicanum* embroideries, Turkish Ottoman and later textiles, simple sprays of blossom being enclosed within a symmetrical framework of branches with tulips and irises either side of the central palmette motif (see also figs 102, 104 and 105 for comparable designs).

These extraordinarily precious textiles had a practical purpose and were used as curtains, hung with the narrower panels either side of the *Fruit Garden* panels, in a reception room at Mrs Longyear's home in Brookline, Massachusetts.[33] JL

76

Portière or hanging (one of a pair)
Designed by May Morris, *c.* 1892,
worked by her assistants (probably)
Embroidered motto: 'Growth sed &
blowth med & springeth wod nu'
Silk damask, embroidered with silk,
with silk fringe and cotton lining
Worked in stem stitch, darning stitch,
satin stitch with couching
253.9 x 99 (100 x 39)
Museum of Fine Arts, Boston (1983.160b)
Given in memory of J. S. and Sayde Z.
Gordon from Myron K. and Natalie G. Stone

77

Small Rose embroidery kit (started)

Designed by May Morris, *c.* 1890,

probably purchased *c.* 1900

Coloured silks and ink on cotton

Worked in darning stitch, stem stitch,

long and short stitch and satin stitch

38 x 49.5 (15 x 19 1/2)

V&A (Circ.302–1960) Given by

Miss Vere Roberts

78

Tulip sideboard runner (detail)

Designed by May Morris, 1890

Worked by Lady Couper, 1904

32 x 166 (12 5/8 x 65 3/8)

Worked in stem stitch

V&A (T.157–2016) Given by Jill Ford

Small Rose and *Tulip* are simple designs, eminently suitable for kits to be finished by a home embroiderer. Both motifs, in different formats, however, were also essential elements of ambitious designs for hangings, such as the *Fruit Garden* portière [fig. 76]. Seven orders for *Small Rose* cushion kits are listed in the Day Book, and other drawings and tracings at the V&A Archive of Art and Design show that it was adapted for a chair seat and a footstool.[34] Similarly, *Tulip* was adapted many times after it was first recorded as a table cover exhibited by May at the Arts and Crafts exhibition in 1890.

The soft cotton supplied as ground fabric for the kits, referred to as 'M cloth' in the Day Book, is probably the 'Manchester cloth' mentioned in the *Embroidery Work* catalogue of *c.* 1912.[35] This has a suitably open weave, allowing embroiderers to define the design with stem stitch and cover areas of ground quickly with darning stitch, using the silk threads or 'twist' supplied by Morris & Co. from their Merton Abbey workshops. According to the catalogue, thick twist and floss silk cost 6*d.* per skein, thin twist 4*d.* Thread was also sold by the ounce (20 skeins) or by pound weight. The Day Book reveals that occasionally filoselle, a type of stranded silk, was also used. JL

Battye wall hanging

Designed by May Morris, embroidered
by Frances Battye, *c.* 1890–1900

Coloured silks on canvas

Worked in darning stitch and stem stitch

188 x 296 (74 x 116 ¹/₂)

WMG (F101) Given by Millicent Audrey
Battye and Hylda Frances Maryon Bibby,
1950

Clients of Morris and Co. could order
unique pieces designed specifically to
meet their own tastes and requirements.
This large embroidered panel was
commissioned from the firm by the
wealthy widow Frances Battye and is one
of the largest hangings May ever devised.
The original design is now in the V&A.

Frances Battye was born in 1846,
daughter of James Jenkinson Bibby,
millionaire owner of the Bibby Shipping
Line. In 1866, Frances married barrister
Richard Battye, who died in 1873 leaving
Battye with a young family. The Day Book
records that from her home 28 Great
Cumberland Place in Marylebone, London,
Frances ordered several embroidered
panels during the early 1890s. The size
of this commissioned hanging would
test the skill of any talented embroiderer.
Owing to its scale and the closely worked
embroidery that covers the entire surface
it is possible Frances worked the panel
with some or all of her daughters
Millicent, Hylda, Norah and Marjorie.

Worked primarily in darning stitches
with outlines in stem stitch, the panel
is richly decorated with three trees
surrounded by flowers and a grape
vine. The scene is populated with small
woodland animals such as a squirrel and
a rabbit as well as colourful larger-than-life
birds in flight. The central design is
bordered on two sides by a band of oak
leaves while at top and bottom and wrapped
round the tree trunks are fourteen proverbs
expressed in archaic language. These
include 'Ye earlie birde getteth ye wurm',
'counte not youre croppes till June is
passed' and 'pennye wyse pounde foolyshe'.
The design is personalized by two coats
of arms in the centre – that on the left of
the Battye family, that on the right is as yet
unidentified. The panel remained in the
family until donated to the William Morris
Gallery soon after it opened in 1950 by
Frances's surviving daughters, Millicent
and Hylda. **RB**

81

A Fruit Garden design

May Morris, 1888

Inscribed 'A Fruit Garden' in May's handwriting and '4'6" x 9'9"/ MORRIS & COMPANY 449 Oxford Street London W'

Watercolour, ink and pencil on paper

33.3 x 20.4 (13¹/₈ x 8)

WMG (D294 vi)

Theodosia Middlemore, a regular Morris & Co. client, ordered the kit for this portière in April 1893.[36] The cost was £9, compared to the finished hangings ordered by Mary Monro Longyear, which were priced at about £47 each [see fig. 74]. The Day Book records that the silk ground was 'lined', presumably owing to the delicacy of the plain woven silk used. Her order was ready on 16 May and probably sent to her home in Birmingham where Theodosia finished the embroidery and signed it in dark red silk thread a year or so later. Remarkably, a photograph (artificially posed) appears to show Theodosia completing the embroidery, which was exhibited in Paris in 1914,[37] and at the exhibition of Victorian and Edwardian Decorative Arts, V&A, 1952, and is now in the permanent collection of the Museum.[38]

This fully worked watercolour design for *Fruit Garden* was originally shown to customers in the Oxford Street shop as a stock design that could be adapted to suit requirements. In addition to the *Fruit Garden* portières illustrated here [figs 74 and 83], the Day Book reveals that a Mrs W. S. Brooks ordered a now untraced pair worked on 'Oak' silk in September 1893.[39] A single portière kit was ordered by Mrs Barr Smith of Adelaide in May 1896, costing £9 plus £1 for the 'motto'. Worked by Mrs Barr Smith's daughter Erlistoun Mitchell, this is still privately owned.[40] In November 1991, a pair worked on pale blue silk was offered at Christie's,[41] and a single example, also on pale blue silk, but with a distinctive long fringe at the hem, was sold in 2009.[42] A further pair, untraced, is recorded in photographs now at the Ashmolean and the V&A,[43] shown hanging in front of a display case apparently containing other textiles. The photograph at the Ashmolean is inscribed in May's handwriting 'Fruit Garden portière on blue silk damask', and initialled 'MM'. JL

82

Theodosia Middlemore embroidering her *Fruit Garden* portière

Photograph, 1893–94

Collection of Stephen Calloway

83

Fruit Garden portière or hanging
Designed by May Morris, 1888
Embroidered by Theodosia Middlemore,
1894
Signed 'Theodosia/1894'
Silk ground embroidered with silk
Worked in darning stitch, stem stitch,
herringbone stitch, buttonhole stitch,
pistil stitch and laid work
Embroidered motto: 'Lo waneth the
Summer the apple boughs fade Yet fair
still my garden twixt sunlight & shade'
275 x 175.5 (108 x 69)
V&A (Circ.206–1965) Purchased from
Rev. Robert Middlemore Bartleet,
Worcestershire

86–89

Bed pelmet and hangings (whole image)

Designed by May Morris, *c*. 1893

Embroidered by May Morris, with
assistants including Maude Deacon,
Ellen Wright and Lily Yeats

Crewel wool on linen

Worked in stem stitch, long and short
stitch, satin stitch, split stitch, chain
stitch, fly stitch and French knots with
laid work

Pelmet 29 x 193 (11³/₈ x 76) (longer
sections), 29 x 139 (11³/₈ x 54³/₄) (shorter
sections); curtains 192 x 122 (75⁵/₈ x 48)

Society of Antiquaries of London:
Kelmscott Manor (KM231.1–3)

Kelmscott Manor provided William Morris
with a real version of the rural utopia he
advocated, and it was a vital part of his
daughter's life. The seventeenth-century
oak four-poster bed in Morris's bedroom
had been made for Thomas Turner, the
farmer who built the house. In the early
1890s, while running the Morris & Co.
workroom, May designed these bed
hangings, incorporating her father's
specially written poem, 'For the bed at
Kelmscott', expressing his appreciation of
the comfort the bed gave. The hangings
were shown at the Arts and Crafts
exhibition in 1893.

The embroidery incorporates typical
Morris elements such as the central
pomegranate tree seen in some of Morris's
earliest embroideries for Red House, and
a trellis background that recalls his first
garden-inspired wallpaper pattern. May's
design, worked mostly with stem, satin,
and long and short stitch with added laid
and couched work, is balanced and unified
yet lively, including sprays of giant poppies
and a total of ten birds, which bring the
eye down to the foreground meadow,
sprinkled with flowers from a medieval
tapestry, and a rabbit sitting at the foot
of the tree. A creeping tendril of giant
stylized flower heads and leaves worked
in greyish green and blue wool very clearly
shows May's study of seventeenth-century
crewel work, linking the embroidery with
the date of the oak frame of the bed itself.

As a family project, the Kelmscott bed
hangings do not appear in the regular orders
listed in the Day Book, but some loose
scraps of paper at the back of the book
referring to the Kelmscott Hangings,
in unknown handwriting, appear to
document the hours and weeks of work
they required, against the initials of May's
assistants. The total cost of the work for
both hangings was over £71.

Mary Sloane's study of Morris's bedroom
[fig. 84] shows the bed draped with the
hangings and the shadowy figure of May
in the doorway. As Julia Dudkiewicz has
suggested (see also the bedcover, fig. 90),
this image indicates the significance of
the bed and its presentation for May's
ongoing work to honour her father's
long-term legacy. The bed and the
hangings were displayed at the V&A's
1934 centenary exhibition, and are still
shown together at Kelmscott Manor
today. JL

84

May Morris in William Morris's
bedroom

Mary Annie Sloane, 1912

Watercolour on paper

23 x 28.5 (9 x 11¹/₄)

WMG (W157) Mary Annie Sloane
bequest, 1962

85
Bed in William Morris's
bedroom, Kelmscott Manor,
with the pelmet and hangings

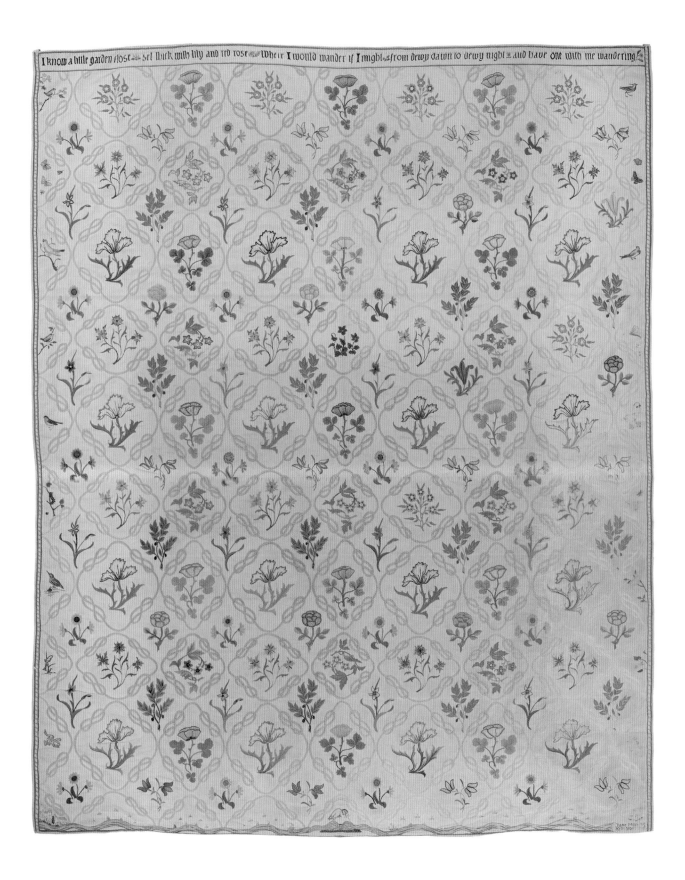

I know a little garden close ⁕ set thick with lily and red rose ⁕ Where I would wander if I might ⁕ from dewy dawn to dewy night ⁕ and have one with me wandering

90–92

Bedcover

Designed by May Morris, *c.* 1910

Worked and signed by Jane Morris

Wool and silk on linen

Worked in stem stitch, chain stitch, long
and short stitch, split stitch, back stitch,
running stitch, with speckling, French
knots, and laid work

Embroidered motto: 'I know a little garden
close/set thick with lily and red rose/
Where I would wander if I might/from
dewy dawn to dewy night/and have one
with me wandering'

261 x 212.5 (102 3/4 x 83 5/8)

Society of Antiquaries of London:
Kelmscott Manor (KM233)

Although currently shown on William
Morris's bed at Kelmscott Manor, this
cover was made after his death, and was
not originally intended for this purpose;
loops stitched to the top edge show that
it was sometimes displayed as a hanging.
Country Life published a photograph of
the cover on Morris's bed in 1921, but
they only became firmly associated after
the 1934 centenary exhibition at the V&A;
correspondence at the Museum shows
that May would have preferred its usual
faded Indian printed cotton cover for
the display.[44]

The pattern reflects May Morris's
knowledge of historic precedents, with
embroidered floral emblems from
the garden at Kelmscott, alternately
contained within a structure of knotwork
compartments stitched with yellow
wool. Although worked with a different
technique, directly onto the linen ground,
these are reminiscent of appliquéd 'slips'
of seventeenth-century embroideries.
Roses, stylized daisies, ragged robin,
parrot tulips, irises, poppies, fritillaries,
rowan branches, and a single clump of
violets are all included, each repeated
almost regularly, but all are unique,
embroidered with different stitches

and colours. Lines from William Morris's
poem 'A Garden by the Sea' from *Poems
by the Way* are stitched across the top
edge of the cover, while a wavy blue river
Thames springs from the centre of the
lower edge, forming a border. Lifelike
studies of small creatures including
butterflies, a caterpillar, and a tiny
depiction of Kelmscott Manor itself,
are embroidered at the two long
sides, designed to be seen vertically.

A coloured preparatory drawing for
a section of a similar bedcover is now
at Kelmscott Manor, and preparatory
drawings of flowers and animals are in the
folders of May's papers at the Ashmolean
Museum. May made a cover to a similar
design in crewel wools on wool for Emery
Walker, still at his house in Hammersmith
today, and a very large version embroidered
with silk on a silk ground, with William
Morris's 1874 *Poppy* border design, was
sold in 2013.[45] JL

94–96

'Melsetter' hangings

Designed by May Morris, 1891–93

Embroidered by May Morris and

Theodosia Middlemore (probably),

c. 1900

Crewel wool thread on hand-woven

linen ground

Worked in stem stitch, satin stitch,

running stitch, fly stitch, speckling, couching

and laid work

191.5 x 146 (75 1/2 x 57 1/2)

National Museums of Scotland

(K.2014.47.1&2)

These embroideries, made for Melsetter House in the Orkney Islands, are the result of close collaboration between May Morris and her friend and client Theodosia Middlemore. They are the only other known examples of hangings worked with May's design for her father's bed hangings [fig. 87]. The coloured wools chosen are chiefly blues, greens and pastel shades, perhaps to reflect the dominance of the sea and sky at Melsetter. The embroideries remained in the Middlemore family until sold in 2013.

Theodosia's husband Thomas Middlemore's saddlery business in Birmingham provided a comfortable living. The couple commissioned significant furnishings from Morris & Co. for their Birmingham home,[46] including a *Fruit Garden* portière [fig. 83]. Theodosia purchased five other embroidery kits from Morris & Co. during the four years covered by the Day Book, including an alms bag, a veil and a burse, the costly gold thread supplied for these showing that she was a skilled and confident embroiderer.

The Middlemores moved to the Orkney island of Hoy in 1896 and commissioned W. R. Lethaby to remodel Melsetter Hall,

work that was completed in 1900. May Morris visited several times, and recalled the impact of the Morris & Co. tapestries and furnishings used to decorate the house: 'a building standing like a fairy-castle in the loneliness of the far North, and filled with all the glow and richness of Morris invention, every room thought out with absolute fitness and beauty by the genius of the Lady-of-the-house'.[47] While at Melsetter May completed several botanical studies for embroidery designs, which are now among her papers at the Ashmolean Museum [see figs 41, 42], as well as a charming design possibly for a personal bookbinding or card case [fig. 93]. Headed with Theodosia's name in large capitals, the design includes personal references and jokes, showing a deer (annotated 'A Dear!') in a landscape representing England, heraldic devices to represent Thomas Middlemore's family, and a tiny figure, presumably May herself, in a sailing boat in stormy seas, heading for Melsetter.

The Middlemores actively supported the community on the island, and the handspun and hand-woven linen ground may have been produced on the estate.[48] As well as spinning, May and Theodosia occupied themselves with dyeing, although it is not clear whether their own wool was used for these hangings. Recent dye analysis completed by the National Museums of Scotland has shown that the coloured wools were produced using both synthetic and natural dyes.[49] It is possible that the two friends each worked one of the hangings; each is unique and surprisingly complex, with individual motifs meticulously planned to differ from their opposites in the other panel. Stems, leaves and birds are worked in regular stem stitches, completely covering the ground, while the large flowers in the foreground use satin stitches, running stitch, speckling, fly stitch, and laid and couched work to

93

'Theodosia' design

May Morris, c. 1900

Pencil and ink on paper

34.4 x 21.5 (13 1/2 x 8 1/2)

Ashmolean Museum (OA1278)

reveal areas of the linen ground as part of the design.

The Melsetter hangings show May's enjoyment and command of the contrasting effects achieved with thick wool thread on a homespun linen. Their effect is dramatically different from the shimmering silk forests of the *Fruit Garden* embroideries [see figs 74, 76], but they are equally significant evidence of May's artistic and technical abilities. JL

97

Vine Leaf table cover

Designed by May Morris, 1896, possibly
made by Mary Hodson, *c.* 1896 or later

Silk thread on linen ground, silk lining

Worked in darning stitch, stem stitch
and satin stitch

108 x 108 (42 ¹/₂ x 42 ¹/₂)

V&A (T.426–1993) Given by Mr and Mrs
L. G. Hodson

Vine leaves and tendrils, carnations, roses,
tulips and poppies are depicted in this
table cover, framed by a cream border
with a circular pattern and lined with blue
silk. The whole of the textile is filled with
darning stitch, worked horizontally for the
background and following the 'curves and
forms of the design' in treating the flowers
and other natural growths.[50] Stem stitch
outlines each central motif. The poppy
pistil is worked in satin stitch, as are some
elements of the circles on the border.
The overall design consists of a quartered
pattern repeat. The design, although
depicting the flowers of an English garden,
also evokes exoticism: the vine tendrils
seemingly mimic Celtic knots, the tulip
ogees are reminiscent of Persian floral
representations and the *mon*-like circular
patterns are found in Japanese designs.
The faded tones, particularly in the centre,
illustrate dyeing variations in what was
once a consistent blue ground.

Laurence and Mary Elizabeth Hodson,
the original owners of this piece,
commissioned Morris & Co. to refurbish
their home, Compton Hall, Staffordshire,
during the 1890s.[51] According to the Day
Book, Mrs Hodson placed at least three
orders for panels to embroider at home
between October 1893 and November
1896: *Apple Tree*, *Daisy and Myrtle* and
Anemone, all worked on her 'own linen',
and avoiding the much higher cost
of a finished Morris & Co. embroidery.
Confusingly, several other orders were
made by Mrs R. W. Hudson, who was also
furnishing a new house in the early 1890s
(see p. 164).[52]

The table cover matches a paper design,
transcribed as 'Vine Leaf Table Cover 1'.
The title and Hodson provenance help
ascertain a likely date of production, as
the design first appears in the Day Book
in March 1896. From then until August
four orders for five *Vine Leaf* table cloths/
covers were placed by the Morris & Co.
Oxford Street shop, all marked as 'started'
and priced from £1. 10s. to £3 depending
on materials and possibly size. Mrs Hodson
may have purchased one of these kits
from the shop, as no *Vine Leaf* design
is recorded in any order placed by her
in the Day Book. HF

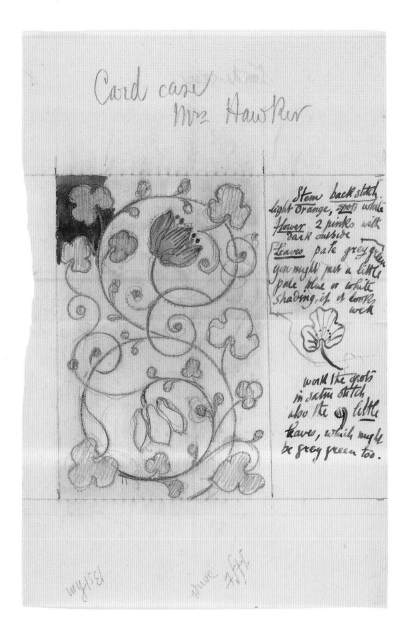

99
'Lotus' panel or curtain (one of a pair), detail
Designed by May Morris (probably)
Embroidered by Morris & Co. (probably),
c. 1895
Coloured silk thread on silk
Worked in darning stitch, satin stitch and
long and short stitch
225 x 119 (88 1/2 x 46 3/4)
V&A (T.364–1976) Given by Mrs
Barrington Haynes

This unusual hanging (and its pair),
initially used as curtains, are worked
almost entirely in darning stitch on a fine
peach-coloured silk. Satin and long and
short stitches are sparingly used on flowers
to add texture. Some areas and lines are
deliberately left unstitched to create shading.

The simple stitches make great impact
when used to work the bold design of
closed and open lotus flowers, fronds
of acanthus, peonies and stylized flowers.
Some of these motifs are also in the *Lotus*
hanging designed by William Morris in
the late 1870s.[54] JL

98
Design for card case
May Morris, 1896
Pencil, ink and watercolour on
tracing paper
20.3 x 13.3 (8 x 5 1/4)
Ashmolean Museum (WA1941.108.39),
1941

Listed in the Day Book in 1896, this design
was ordered by a Mrs Hawker. May's
annotations include instructions on stitches
and colours to be used. The design was
started in fine twisted silk and sent to the
client to complete at home. May exhibited
two untraced card cases at the 1906 Arts
and Crafts exhibition, described as *Silver
Rose* and *An Eastern Garden*. They were
illustrated in *The Studio*, along with an
intricate white velvet cushion embroidered
with birds and vine leaves.[53] AM

100

Panels for *Owl* three-fold screen
Designed by May Morris, probably in 1896
Coloured silks on silk
Worked in darning stitch and stem stitch
68 x 37.5 (26 ³/₄ x 14 ³/₄) (each panel)
Private collection

The Day Book contains a note dated
13 July 1896, addressed to May (as Mrs
Sparling) on Morris & Co. headed paper,
asking for an estimate of the cost of
design and materials for three small
screens each measuring 68.6 x 38.1 cm
(27 x 15 ins). Written by a now unknown
employee, the note continues 'the chief
point...is that "owls" are to form part
of the design (on silk would perhaps give
less work) will you please write by return
stating cost of design starting work'.
May's reply was then noted: '£5 – darned
thk [thick] twist'. This illustrates
communications between the shop
and May while she was in charge of
the embroidery business, and almost
definitely refers to these small panels.[55]
Working the design on a pale blue silk
increases the richness of the effect,
although it is unlikely to have entailed less
work, because of the delicacy of the fabric.

The design of the panels, which may
have been developed through more detailed
requests from the client, tells the story of
a single owl on a small oak sapling, with
daffodils growing below. He (or she) looks
excited as another owl joins the tree on an
opposite branch, turning its back, in the
second panel, this time with bluebell-like
flowers. Finally the two owls both face
outwards, above a row of red tulips. Each
tree is worked with subtly different shades
of green, adding a few more leaves, and a
twining frond of ivy grows strong and dark
by the third panel. While unmistakably
designed within the familiar Morris & Co.
framework, this series shows May's
originality and humour, using colour and
stitches to convey narrative and the passing
of time. **JL**

'Spring and Summer' panel
Designed and probably embroidered
by May Morris, 1895–1900
Coloured silks on silk damask
Worked in coloured silks and metal
thread with laid and couched work, French
knots, running, long and short stitches,
back stitch, split stitch, satin stitch and
stem stitch
Embroidered motto 'Quant li estes et la
douce saison fait foelle et fleurs et le pres
raverdir' ('When the summer's gentle
season makes leaves and flowers and
fields green again')
130.8 x 71.8 (51 $\frac{1}{2}$ x 28 $\frac{1}{4}$)
Private collection

The ability to capture nature, whether
countryside flowers, animals and particularly
birds, was key to the development of May's
work as she moved away from the Morris
& Co. style. In this exquisite embroidery,
celebrating the cycle of the seasons, two

large parakeets and four pairs of more
familiar birds, perfectly worked in silk
thread, are full of life, yet they also
function as formal elements, emphasizing
the symmetrical arrangement of twining
stems, leaves and flowers.

In the first of this set of two hangings,
roundels in each corner of the upper section
depict a blossoming tree in spring and a
lily in full flower for summer, either side
of a swirling pool of silk-embroidered fish,
and above a quotation from a song by
twelfth-century troubadour Chatelaine de
Coucy. Otherwise identical, the companion
piece [figs 103, 104] has roundels with an
autumnal vine ripe with grapes, and a
sparse olive tree for winter. In both panels,
the upper section is surrounded by a band
of regular lattice work of couched floss
silk, and each is meticulously stitched
throughout.

The main design of the panels is
centred on a formal group of stylized
roses, twining with sprays of tulips,
suggestive of the Turkish textiles that
provided inspiration for many Morris & Co.
patterns. These flowers are contained

by twining stems of couched gold thread,
which spring from two vines extending
from the lower corners, a design directly
inspired by medieval embroideries
illustrating the Tree of Jesse, which
represent figures from Christ's ancestry
in similar compartments.[56] The medieval
embroideries often also include vine
leaves worked in metal thread, which
May reinterprets here. The foreground
is worked with small clumps of flowers,
reminiscent of medieval tapestries. May's
design successfully unites historic, natural
and geometric forms, even including small
areas of abstract blue shading representing
water or clouds, suggesting the imagery
of East Asian textiles, and creating highly
original and distinctive works. The 'Oak'
silk damask ground, with its secondary
pattern, unifies and adds additional depth
to the arrangement.

The panels were undoubtedly a very
special commission, although it is not
currently known for whom they were made.
It is possible, however, that they were the
'2 panels for Cabinet, specially designed',
an order for a Mrs Mawns, recorded in
the Day Book by May on 29 August 1894.
These cost £150, the most expensive order
in the book, a price that may have included
the cabinet itself. There is evidence that the
embroideries were originally mounted in
a glass frame or cabinet door, as there
is a narrow unworked border around each
edge, and their size also suggests that this
proposal is not unreasonable.

The collection of May's papers at the
Ashmolean Museum includes some
preparatory drawings for these panels,
as well as a working drawing [fig. 105] for
a different, much larger portière. This also
incorporates pairs of birds and vine leaf
compartments enclosing flowers, although
in a simpler format. The drawing has rough
workings and notes, suggesting that the
design could be adapted for a table cover,
although this seems an unlikely use for
such a vertical design. JL

103 and 104

'Autumn and Winter' panel

Designed and probably embroidered

by May Morris, 1895–1900

Embroidered motto 'et les dous chans des

menus oisillons fait les pluiseurs de joie

souvenir' ('and the gentle song of little

birds recalls joyful memories')

Coloured silks on silk damask

Worked in coloured silks and metal

thread with laid and couched work, French

knots, running, long and short stitches,

back stitch, split stitch, satin stitch and

stem stitch

130.8 x 71.8 (51 1/2 x 28 1/4)

Private collection

105

Design or working drawing for a portière

May Morris, *c.* 1895

Pencil, ink and watercolour on paper

35 x 24.7 (13 3/4 x 9 3/4)

Ashmolean Museum (WA1941.108.43),

1941

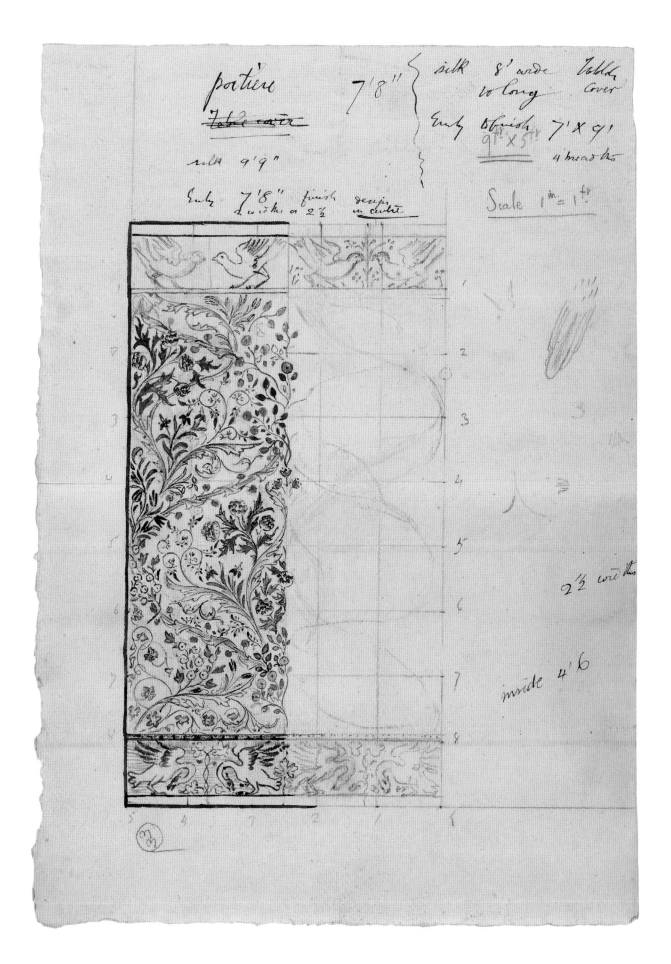

106

The Homestead and the Forest cot quilt

Designed by May Morris

Embroidered by Jane Morris, 1889–90

Silks on a linen and silk mix ground

Worked in darning stitch, running stitch, stem stitch, satin stitch and herringbone stitch, trellis and French knots

153 x 126 (60 $^1/_4$ x 49 $^5/_8$)

Society of Antiquaries of London: Kelmscott Manor (KM612) Purchased by May Elliot Hobbs from the Kelmscott Manor sale July 1939, lot 162, and thence by descent; purchased by the Society of Antiquaries, 2016

A collaboration between mother and daughter in the months leading up to May's wedding, this delightful quilt was probably intended for a child of her own. It remained in May's possession until the end of her life and was one of the treasures she showed visitors at Kelmscott Manor.[57] First shown in 1890 at the third Arts and Crafts exhibition, it was singled out for praise in the press: 'Perhaps of all the pieces contributed by the Morris family this is one of the best and most original.'[58] The title is inscribed on a handwritten label attached to the reverse; it was also referred to as the 'Beast Quilt' when exhibited in New York in 1910.[59]

At the centre of the quilt is a farmhouse with fruit trees, gardens and domesticated animals. This ordered and cultivated landscape is surrounded by a river with leaping fish, frogs and a sharp-toothed crocodile. Beyond is a wilder terrain with exotic animals, birds and fauna, set against the rays of the sun. As curator Kathy Haslam explains, many of the birds and animals were adapted from engravings by Thomas Bewick, sourced from books in William Morris's library.[60] They form a stitched encyclopaedia of the animal kingdom, designed for parent and child to linger over, identifying and discovering the wonders of the natural world.

The twelve carefully chosen quotations and proverbs bordering the quilt reinforce this pedagogic intent. Taken from a variety of sources, including Plato's *Republic*, the *Rubaiyat* of Omar Khayyam and William Blake's *Songs of Innocence and Experience*, they promote the importance of education, kindness, hard work and fairness, and are quoted in a number of languages, including Farsi, Italian and Latin.[61]

The distinctive format of the design is reminiscent of a medieval world map, or the famous eleventh-century Creation 'tapestry' from Girona.[62] A more exact source may yet come to light – in a lecture on pattern designing May recalled a textile that captured 'all the drama of field and forest and desert place – the sun's rays breaking through a cloud, the eagle flying up to the heavens, the lion with streaming mane, the stag in the fenced park, the pond with its fish and wildfowl, the castle with its boundaries, its woods and gardens'.[63]

Designs for this embroidery survive in the V&A Archive of Art and Design.[64] As Linda Parry has noted, Jane Morris's interpretation of May's design is 'a masterpiece in its application of technique using the minimum of stitches to retain May's own drawing style'.[65] Nearly all the stitches used are described in *Decorative Needlework*, with the exception of the close herringbone stitch on the tulip petals.

This quilt is the most personal and elaborate of a number of cot quilts designed by May. In 1884, May and Jenny collaborated on a cradle cover for the baby son of T. J. and Anne Cobden-Sanderson: 'We hope he will want to pick the flowers and so compliment our work. If it gives you half as much pleasure to receive, as it gave us to work it, we shall be proud indeed.'[66] Cot quilts were also sold commercially through the firm; three designs are listed in the Day Book, of which one, 'an animal cot quilt' started for a Mrs Whitley in 1893, may have been a copy or simplified version of this design. Another version, now lost, is referenced in Margaret Swain's *Figures on Fabric*.[67] **AM**

107 and 108

Minstrel with Cymbals

Adapted from a design by William Morris,
c. 1867

Embroidered by May Morris, possibly
early 1890s

Silks, gold and metal thread on linen

Worked in long and short stitch and split
stitch with couched goldwork

29 x 13.5 (11 3/8 x 5 1/4)

William Morris Society (T088) Donated
by Pamela and Elizabeth Rice in memory
of Patrick Rice, 2012

This embroidery is based on a William
Morris design for stained glass. A collection
of May's lantern slides in the Ruskin &
Morris Center of Osaka, Japan, includes
an image of her design for this panel,
without the detail of the tiled floor. A related
design of a minstrel with harp is in the
Ashmolean Museum.[68] May owned a set
of six Morris & Co. stained-glass panels,
including musical figures that she gifted
to the V&A in 1923.[69] Figurative designs
are rare in May's work; such panels were
probably created to demonstrate her
technical virtuosity on a small scale. At the
1893 Arts and Crafts show May exhibited
'A small figure worked in floss silk, gold
and silver thread', which may be identical
with this panel.[70] **AM**

109

Decorative Needlework

May Morris, 1893

Published by Joseph Hughes & Co.,
London

23 x 19.5 (9 x 7⅝)

WMG (K2682) Donated by Joan
Edwards, 2002

This beginner's guide to embroidery was published when May's reputation in the field was becoming well established. Through her writing as well as her practice, she sought to raise the status of embroidery: 'in spite of the discouraging trifling and dabbling in silks, which is often all that stands for embroidery, I am inclined to take needle-art seriously, and regard its simply priceless decorative qualities worth as careful study or appreciation as any other form of art.'[71] In the early 1890s she contributed chapters on embroidery to Arthur Heygate Mackmurdo's *Plain Handicrafts* (1892) and to the catalogues published by the Arts & Crafts Exhibition Society.[72]

Decorative Needlework was intended as a supplement, rather than as an alternative to practical instruction. May herself offered private embroidery lessons costing half a guinea each, which included materials for practising with; instruction in church and other 'elaborate frame embroidery' cost more.[73] No doubt the publication of *Decorative Needlework* was partly motivated by a desire to enhance her teaching credentials. As an instructor, May comes across clearly, giving gentle encouragement and urging would-be students to practise simplicity in all things if they want to produce work that has 'life and meaning'.

The text is critical of the impact that the fast pace of modern life and cheap machine-work have had on the practice of embroidery. There are hints of May's

socialist beliefs in a rebuke to those who wear dainty embroidered clothes without valuing the labour involved, 'wrought by what under-paid work-girl she does not know or care'.[74] May advises readers to avoid modern work and study the South Kensington (V&A) Museum's collection of early English medieval embroideries, known as *opus anglicanum*, on which she became an authority. *Decorative Needlework* is illustrated with a detail from the *Tree of Jesse* cope (1310–25), a work described as 'instinct with life and originality'.[75] May promotes medieval work not for readers to copy slavishly, but to be inspired by the artistic possibilities of embroidery.

As a teaching manual, *Decorative Needlework* combines practical instruction with a clearly argued philosophy of what makes the art of embroidery distinctive and worthwhile. Different stitches are categorized according to whether worked loose in the hand or on a frame. The descriptions are accompanied by illustrations and evocative accounts of how the stitches have been applied on different historic textiles. This lends the narrative colour, preventing it from being a merely technical manual. Some of the textiles described relate to Indian and Iranian embroideries that belonged to the Morris family.[76] May owned a small collection of eastern and European textiles, possibly inherited from her father, that she used for research and teaching. Some are preserved in Birmingham Museum and Art Gallery and include a fine panel of nineteenth-century Resht work of the type described in *Decorative Needlework*.[77]

For May, good design was of paramount importance: 'While inferior work can be tolerated for the sake of the design, if that is good...excellent work on a worthless design must be cast aside as labour lost... design is the very soul and essence of beautiful embroidery.'[78] May encouraged her readers to make careful studies of

plants and flowers as the only way to understand natural forms. However, she made a clear distinction between studies and design, which should 'merely recall nature, not absolutely copy it; the living flower should inspire a living ornament... certain characteristics being dwelt upon, but the forms all simplified, leaves flatly arranged, stems bent into flowing curves to fill the required spaces'.[79] She insists on the decorative qualities of embroidery and the need for symmetry, balance and order. As William Morris also argued in his lecture 'Hints on Pattern Designing', there must be nothing vague; a designer must understand every line he/she draws and 'be definite before everything'.[80]

May applied the same principles to colour, advocating a limited palette of pure bright shades, harmoniously combined. She defended the use of bright colours despite the fashion for muted shades, urging her readers to 'avoid like poison the yellowish-brown green of a sickly hue that professes to be "artistic"'.[81] She was strongly opposed to the art of needle painting, that is the attempt to imitate in stitch the thousands of shades found in nature 'till a libellous caricature of natural growth is achieved'.[82] In her view, the decorative qualities of embroidery required the use of flat, simple colours with limited shading, and she shared her father's enthusiasm for natural, as opposed to chemical, dyes.

May designed the binding for *Decorative Needlework*, with a repeat pattern of flower sprays and a roundel to contain the lettering. The cover design was blocked in gold on 125 special copies. Both issues were printed on large uncut paper with very wide margins. As the 'Publisher's Circular' from 3 June 1893 explained, 'There is plenty of room in the margins of the pages for notes, if the fair readers should wish to make any.'[83] **AM**

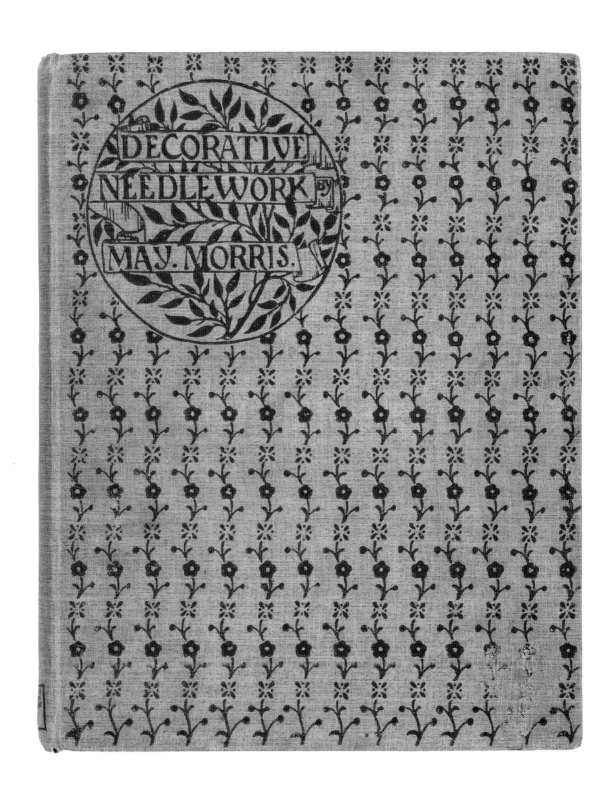

110–113

Notes and sketches for embroidery
lectures
May Morris, c. 1899–1902
Ink and pencil on paper
Various sizes
WMG (J561) Given by the V&A from
the gift of Dr Robert Steele, 1955

These lecture notes (a total of sixteen
loose sheets) date from May's time
teaching embroidery at the Birmingham
Municipal School of Art and the Central
School of Arts and Crafts.[84] Echoing
many of the ideas expressed in *Decorative
Needlework*, they served as an aide-
memoire for her practical classes, covering
design, technique and materials. May
urged simplicity, cautioning against the
'danger of overshading' and reminding
students to 'make your spaces interesting,
for restraint tells as much as profusion –
more'.[85] **AM**

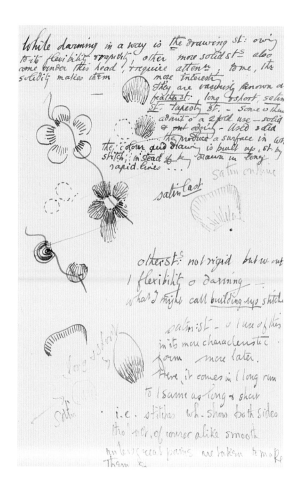

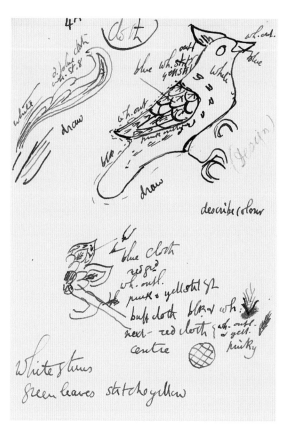

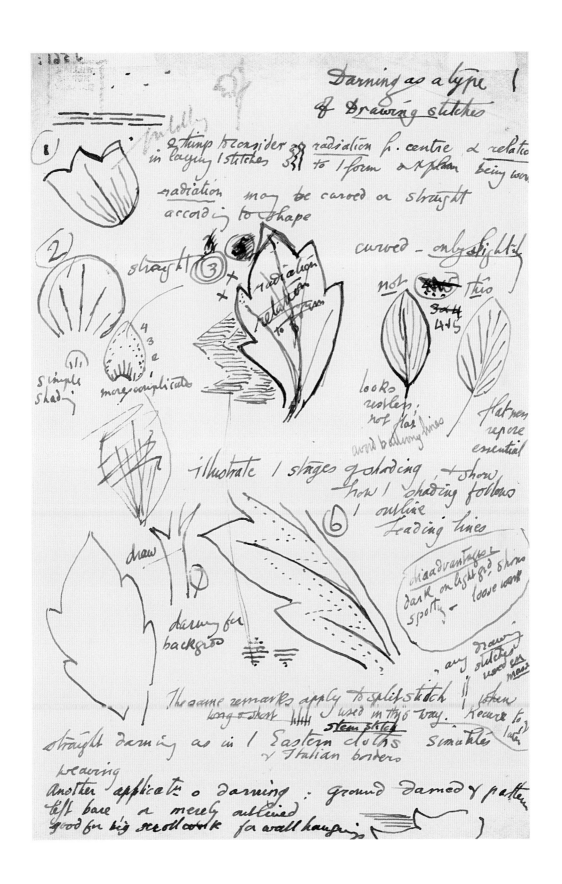

Darning as a type
of Drawing stitches

2 things to consider as radiation fr. centre & relation
in laying 1 stitches to 1 form or plane being work

radiation may be curved or straight
according to shape

straight curved — only slightly

radiation not this
relation
to

simple more complicated looks
shading restless,
not flat
avoid bubbling lines

flat men
repose
essential

illustrate 1 stages of shading, + show
how 1 shading follows
1 outline
leading lines

draw disadvantages
dark on light gd, shows
spotty - loose work

darning for
backgro any drawing
stitches
used

The same remarks apply to split stitch when
long o short used in this way. Recur to later
stem stitch

straight darning as in 1 Eastern cloths similarly
& Italian borders
weaving

Another application o darning: ground darned & pattern
left bare or merely outlined
good for big scroll work for wall hangings

114

Vine panel

Designed by May Morris or Philip Webb

Worked by May Morris, 1885–90

Linen canvas embroidered with silk

Worked in cross stitch, tent stitch

and condensed Scotch stitch

65.4 x 65.4 (25³/₄ x 25³/₄)

V&A (T.69–1939) Bequeathed by

May Morris

William Morris disapproved of canvas and cross-stitch embroidery as being repetitive and mechanical, leading to a loss of artistic skills. May apparently 'despised' the technique [see fig. 137], although this panel remained among her possessions until she died. It is worked in a range of canvas-work stitches and is reminiscent of seventeenth-century English needlework. The motif of the central stylized tree with vine leaves suggests a possible connection to church embroideries. JL

115

Orange Tree panel
Designed and embroidered by
May Morris, possibly c. 1897
Silks on linen
Worked in long and short stitch,
stem stitch and French knots
41.8 x 43.5 (16 1/2 x 17 1/8)
William Morris Society (T33) Bequeathed
by Helena Stephenson, 1970

This embroidery appears to be unique; it does not match any description in the Day Book. The distinctive leaves, with a 'heart-shaped' base, come from a variety of sour orange that May sketched in Egypt in 1897.[86] As described in *Decorative Needlework*, most of the leaves are worked in two shades, one half dark the other light, with a firm outline to render the pattern clear. The oranges are worked from the centre outwards in bright shades of silk that stand out against the blue ground. Orange blossom was a popular bridal flower; possibly this panel was given or commissioned as a wedding gift. **AM**

116

Design for a super-frontal for an altar

Philip Webb, 1898–99

Pencil, ink and watercolour on paper

51.4 x 76.3 (20 $\frac{1}{4}$ x 30)

Signed and dated with extensive
technical notes

V&A (E.58–1940) Bequeathed by
May Morris

117

Super-frontal

Designed by Philip Webb, 1898–99

Embroidered by May Morris

Coloured silk and gold thread, probably
on linen. Attached to a frontal or panel
of blue linen

Worked in long and short stitch, stem
stitch, split stitch, French knots, laid work
with Bayeux stitch and couched goldwork

34.9 x 145.4 (13 $\frac{3}{4}$ x 57 $\frac{1}{4}$) (embroidered
section only)

V&A (T.379–1970) Given by the Rochester
and Southwark Diocesan Deaconess
House

This super-frontal was ordered by William Morris's sister, Isabella Gilmore, leader of the Rochester and Southwark Diocesan Deaconess House, the Anglican community in Clapham, South London, who commissioned Philip Webb to design a chapel and a simple altar table.[87] The super-frontal, used to decorate the altar for church festivals, demonstrates Webb's technical knowledge of embroidery work and his strong belief in the ability of May to execute his design to the highest standard.

The full-size coloured drawing by Webb of half of the design was left to the V&A by May Morris many years before the super-frontal and the altar table itself were given to the Museum. The drawing is carefully annotated with instructions, which indicate that the top of the frontal was to be red velvet. Instead of working the very detailed, close pattern in gold and silk thread directly onto the velvet, Webb suggests working the red ground of the design in silk to match the velvet, a more practical approach; May chose to work it in long and short stitch. He also gives detailed notes on colours to be used, requesting that the effect of one of the borders is to be like 'glass jewels'. The design, of five crosses worked in couched gold thread, has meandering vines and oak leaves in laid work with Bayeux stitch, with borders and details worked with split stitch, stem stitch and French knots.

A handwritten note, possibly by Isabella Gilmore, attached to the frontal relates the first-person story of its making: 'Philip Webb delighted to give the design for me to May, he said the only woman in England who could work it for me.' The note also describes how the frontal travelled to Paris in 1914 for exhibition, was 'rushed down to the Great Cellars at the Louvre and walled up', and could not return until 1919, after the end of the First World War. JL

Full size coloured drawing of Labelled altar Cloth super frontal - coloured.
The length here given is one half the length of altar.

Notes   Before cutting the stuff, the top of the altar should be exactly measured, as the pattern was made from the original drawing of the altar, and the wood-work may not have been quite correct in its dimensions.

Suggestions   As I gathered there might be some difficulty in working this close pattern in the gold and silks on the velvet, I might be easier and better first to get the velvet, or nearer to the desired colour as possible, for the top of altar, and then to fill in the ground with wools worked after the same depths and tone as the velvet.

In tracing of the whole length of the super frontal, there has been no designed that none of the leafage &c. is repeated, though the whole is arranged in the same system of design.

Care should be taken in the colouring of the continuous line of border B which should look like glass jewels. The red should be full coloured and bright; the green bright leaf colour; the blue greyish in colour and not harsh.

The border line A should be deep indigo blue, and the alternate spiral beading should be light straw coloured white.

Notes continued   The middle part of border, C, should have its ground filled in with a grern brown, and the netline & leafage &c should be black not blue.

Care should be taken that the blue ground, on which the embroidered gold thread cross is laid, should be a real blue, of silver-grey quality.

In cutting the stuff for work, allow for shrinkage caused by the pull of the embroidery.

K. V
1895 - 99

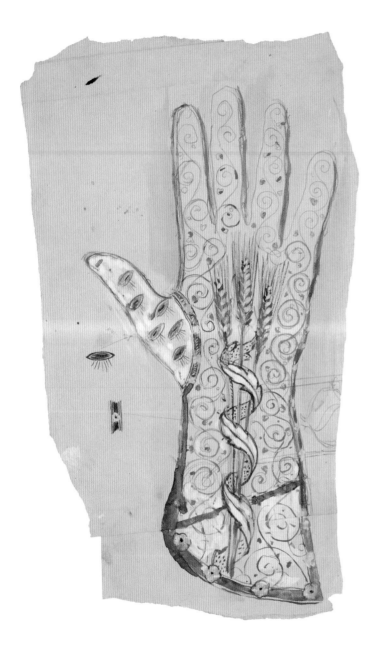

118

Design or working drawing

After design by Charles Ricketts, c. 1899

Pencil and watercolour on paper

20.5 x 34 (8 x 13 3/8)

Ashmolean Museum (OA1285)

119

Glove, one of a pair sometimes known
as the 'Easter' or the 'Bishop's' gloves

Designed by Charles Ricketts, c. 1899

Embroidered by May Morris

Coloured silk and applied gold braid on linen

Worked in chain stitch, satin stitch,
stem stitch, speckling, herringbone stitch,
back stitch and couching

Length 35 (13 3/4)

V&A (T.71&A–1939) Bequeathed by
May Morris

These gloves were exhibited at least three
times during May's lifetime: in the 1899
Arts and Crafts exhibition; in New York in
1910; and in Paris in 1914.[88] The catalogue
entries for the 1910 and 1914 exhibitions
clearly state Ricketts (artist, sculptor, writer
and theatre designer) as the designer,
although the final pattern for the gloves
is likely to have been completed in close
collaboration with the embroiderer. There
is no evidence that the gloves were ever
used in a church, however, and they came
to the V&A as part of May Morris's estate.
The design reflects May's interest in late
sixteenth- and early seventeenth-century
English embroidery. The gloves are worked
in a large number of stitches and the
borders of applied gold braid are worked
with satin-stitched flower heads, with tiny
seed pearls. Each glove has a drop tassel
worked over with needle lace. Two design
drawings and a tracing at the Ashmolean
Museum[89] show different stages in the
process of making the gloves, and also
show that they were initially designed with
a patterned thumb, never actually worked. JL

120

Mittens

Designed by Charles Ricketts

Embroidered by May Morris, 1905–6

Coloured silk and applied gold braid
on linen

Worked in satin stitch, split stitch,
tent stitch and couching

7.5 (3) (width) x 8.2 (3 1/4) (length)

V&A (T.23&A–1958) Given by Riette
Sturge Moore

These tiny mittens, also inspired by
Elizabethan embroidery, are worked with
butterflies, leaves and flowers with satin
stitch, split stitch, couching, tent stitch,
finished with floss silk rosettes and
strawberry drops made of beads covered
with silk worked with needle lace and
running stitch pips.

The mittens were made for the
christening of Daniel Sturge Moore,
son of Thomas Sturge Moore, illustrator,
wood engraver and poet, a close associate
of Charles Ricketts.[90] The gloves were
exhibited at the Glasgow School of Art's
exhibition of Ancient and Modern
Embroidery and Needlecraft (no. 412)
in 1916, and given to the V&A by Daniel
Sturge Moore's daughter in a tiny glass
display case. JL

LEFT

121

Tablecloth (detail)

May Morris and Marianne Collins

109 x 102 (42 7/8 x 40 1/8)

1895–1904

Coloured silks and whitework on cotton

Worked with drawn thread work, stem,

satin and long and short stitches

Society of Antiquaries of London:

Kelmscott Manor (KM214) Given by

Ada Browett, 1977

According to donor Ada Browett, former student at Birmingham School of Art, this tablecloth was jointly worked by May and Marianne Collins, who was also a student at Birmingham during May's time teaching there. Browett stated that the piece won a prize in the Royal School of Art Needlework competition. The combination of whitework and stylized rosehips in coloured silks is unusual compared to May's other designs from this time and perhaps shows Collins' influence in the overall design. **RB**

OPPOSITE

122

Owl hanging or bedcover

The students and teachers of the

Birmingham School of Art, *c.* 1905–06

Wool on Harris linen

Worked with stitches including long and

short stitch, laid work, stem stitch, satin

stitch, darning stitch and French knots

212 x 155 (83 1/2 x 61)

Birmingham City University (2003.0458)

May lectured at Birmingham School of Art from 1895, before starting more formal teaching there in 1899.[91] Here she met Mary Newill, an accomplished designer whose embroidery style is evident in this large panel. It was exhibited at the 1906 Arts and Crafts exhibition and the New Zealand International Exhibition, 1906–07.[92] **RB**

123

Embroidery design

May Morris, *c.* 1900–10

Watercolour and pencil on paper

50.2 x 21.6 (19 3/4 x 8 1/2)

V&A (E.50–1940) Bequeathed by
May Morris

The intricate details of the ground of
this distinctive design may relate to
a printed textile, which May intended
to embroider over in the coloured areas.
The strong twisting lines are reminiscent
of seventeenth-century models, whereas
the small stylized flowers are characteristic
of May's own style. This working drawing,
probably unfinished, is clearly a small
section of a larger design. JL

124

Embroidery design

May Morris, *c.* 1910

Pencil, ink and watercolour on calico

39 x 57.5 (15 3/8 x 22 5/8)

V&A (E.957–1954) Bequeathed by
May Morris

These two designs [figs 124, 125] reflect
May's interest in historic needlework. The
design for a 'Sofa back' [fig. 125] is inspired
by patterns found in English monochrome
and polychrome embroidery of the late
sixteenth and early seventeenth centuries.
The choice of blue and black coloured
silks recalls mid-eighteenth-century
American colonial needlework stitched
in indigo-dyed threads, a style revived in
1896 by the Blue and White Society of
Historic Deerfield in Massachusetts.[93]
It is possible that May saw the Historic
Deerfield work during her American tour.
  The embroidered cloth [fig. 126] is one
of a group of three embroideries finished
in a similar style, all originally purchased
from the Kelmscott Manor sale in 1939. JL

125

Embroidery design, annotated 'Sofa back'

May Morris, *c.* 1910

Pencil and watercolour on paper

27.5 x 25.2 (10³/₄ x 9⁷/₈)

V&A (E.46–1940) Bequeathed by

May Morris

126

Sofa back

Designed by and probably embroidered

by May Morris, *c.* 1910

Coloured silks on linen

Worked in chain stitch, long and short

stitch, stem stitch, back stitch and

buttonhole stitch

49 x 77 (19¹/₄ x 30¹/₄)

Crafts Study Centre, University for the

Creative Arts, Farnham (T.87.1) Donated

by Robin and Heather Tanner

The frieze shows embroidered Gothic script reading: "See we have left our hopes and fears behind & to give our very hearts up unto thee & What better place than this then... could we find by this sweet stream that knows not of the sea & that guesses not the city's misery & This little stream... whose ba... have nar... far off lo... of the T..."

ABOVE

127

June frieze

Designed and embroidered by

May Morris, *c.* 1909–10

Initialled 'MM'

Wools on linen

Worked in split stitch, chain stitch,

stem stitch, satin stitch, long and

short stitch and French knots

70.5 x 278.7 (27³/₄ x 109³/₄)

WMG (F102) Purchased from

Sir Sydney Cockerell, 1951

Simply embroidered in wools on a coarse linen ground, this frieze evokes a hazy hot day in early summer and stands tribute to May's love of Kelmscott and the surrounding countryside. At the centre of the panel is a small landscape impression of the Manor, viewed from across the banks of the Thames and worked in long and short stitch. The ground is dotted with flowers, including clumps of springy heather, strawberries, roses, violets and fritillaries. Butterflies, birds and even a little snail animate the scene. May was a keen gardener and her letters are full of references to the pleasure she took in the flowers and wildlife at Kelmscott.

The verses were carefully chosen from the 'June' poem in William Morris's *The Earthly Paradise*, with additional lines from a May-day verse by the poet and literary critic Sir Walter Alexander Raleigh (1861–1922). Worked in Gothic script, the lines are separated by single leaf and flower motifs that recall the punctuation ornaments in Morris's Kelmscott Press books. The frieze is initialled 'MM' in the lower right corner. The colours were once much more vibrant; the wools that May used faded quickly, much to her displeasure.[94]

May designed this embroidery for her London home at 8 Hammersmith Terrace shortly before she began editing her father's literary works. During these years she split her time between Hammersmith and Kelmscott, often visiting the Manor for extended periods of work as well as rest. Country life was not always the idyll evoked by this embroidery. The Manor could be bitterly cold in winter, subject to floods and lacking many creature comforts; however, May always referred to it with a sense of homecoming. The embroidery offered a pleasant reminder that the river Thames, which flowed past the end of the garden at Hammersmith Terrace, was connected to Kelmscott. The frieze was hung against Morris's

Though our songs cannot banish ancient wrongs Though they follow where the rose goes And their sound swooning over hollow ground fade and leave the enchanted air bare Yet the wise say that not unblest he dies who has known a single may & day

Willow Bough wallpaper, also chosen for the 'pleasant river-scenes' at Kelmscott it recalled.[95] This embroidery is probably the 'Kelmscott hanging' exhibited in New York in 1910.

Lack of funds, caused partly by expensive repairs required at Kelmscott Manor, forced May to give up her London home in 1923 and move permanently to the country. She sold or gave away many London possessions and this embroidery was gifted to Sydney Cockerell, co-trustee of the Morris estate. Correspondence provides the dating of the embroidery and other interesting insights, such as May's instruction on cleaning: 'I was sorry to send the little hanging in such a grubby condition: I believe I should try dry cleaning. If washed at home, it would need a lot of rain-water and doing it oneself very swiftly and intelligently so that the colours should not run – I mean ordinary servants would not do it properly.'[96] **AM**

ABOVE
128
The embroidery *in situ* at
8 Hammersmith Terrace, V&A

129

The heavens declare... panel

Designed and embroidered by
May Morris, probably 1910s

Signed 'MM'

Wools on linen

Worked in split stitch, long and short
stitch, satin stitch and fly stitch

75 × 141.5 (29 1/2 × 55 3/4)

Society of Antiquaries of London:
Kelmscott Manor (KM153) Given by
E. S. McHarg, 1980s

Signed with May's initials in the lower
right corner, this embroidery has a style
of lettering very similar to that in fig. 127.
The inscription is from Psalm 19:1 and
the wide unworked area of linen at the
bottom of the hanging suggests that
it may have been a reredos, designed
to hang behind a small altar table. The
embroidery was reputedly given by May
to Lady Mactaggart, the second wife of
Sir John Auld Mactaggart, around 1928.
Sir John was a property developer and
admirer of William Morris. The couple
lived in an Arts and Crafts villa named
Kelmscott on Sprinkell Avenue,
Shawlands, in Glasgow.[97] **AM**

130

Vine hanging or portière

Designed by William Morris, possibly

c. 1878

Embroidered by May Morris and others

(probably, Wilhelmina Edelstein), *c.* 1916

Coloured silks on linen

Worked in stem stitch, satin stitch,

long and short stitch and chain stitch

249 x 155 (98 x 61)

V&A (T.67–1939) Bequeathed by

May Morris

131

Embroidery Work

Published by Morris & Co., London,

c. 1912

Paper and ink

28.4 x 22.6 (11 x 9)

William Morris Gallery (J2169) Given

by Kathleen Wells, 1957

The portière was a versatile design, illustrated in the *Embroidery Work* catalogue of *c.* 1912 [fig. 131] as a door hanging worked in muted blues and green wools in response to the demand for fashionable recreations of woollen crewel work embroidery of the seventeenth and eighteenth centuries. This version, in contrast, is worked in vivid but complementary shades of grape, plum and pink silks, chiefly in outline, increasing the impact of the vibrant yellow ground. In 1892, May wrote specifically about the care needed when combining shades of yellow with purple, recommending a 'purple very dusky and dead in tone and yellow clear and fresh; the least tendency to a "buttery" shade on the one hand and a hot red purple on the other makes the most ingeniously hideous admixture of colour possible to imagine'.[98] This is likely to be the *Vine* hanging on yellow linen shown at the 1916 Arts and Crafts exhibition.[99] JL

MORRIS EMBROIDERIES.

"VINE" EMBROIDERED PORTIÈRE OR WALL HANGING IN "MORRIS" TAPESTRY WOOLS.

Messrs. Morris's Embroidery Designs are protected, and must in no circumstances be copied.

Pair of bed hangings
Designed by May Morris
Embroidered by May Morris, Mary Newill,
Dora Webb, G. Cattell, A. B. Simpson,
Isobel Catterson-Smith, Mrs Moore,
Nan Hornby, M. Dalton and Wilhelmina
Edelstein, 1916
Wools on linen
Stitches include stem stitch, long and
short stitch, running stitch and speckling
195 x 68.6 (76 3/4 x 27)
Cranbrook Art Museum, Michigan
(CAM 1955.402) Gift of George Gough
Booth and Ellen Scripps Booth, 1955

These brightly coloured curtains were part
of a set of bed hangings designed for the
Arts and Crafts exhibition at the Royal
Academy in 1916. Despite challenging
wartime conditions, the show was one of
the largest ever mounted. May collaborated
with fellow craftsman Ernest Gimson
(1864–1919) and the Women's Guild of
Arts on two separate decorative schemes.[100]
These hangings were displayed in 'a lady's
bedroom' furnished by the Guild, on a
bedstead made at Sapperton in the
Cotswolds. May was also involved in
decorating some of the bedroom furniture,
painted in vermilion thus creating a brilliant
effect against the hangings.

The hangings were embroidered by May
and her friend and former colleague Mary
Newill, with assistance from students
at the Birmingham School of Art and
Wilhelmina Edelstein, student at the
Hammersmith School of Arts and Crafts
where May was an advisor.[101] As the
exhibition catalogue pointed out, 'most
of the wools...were dyed under William
Morris's direction', thus using natural not
chemical dyes.[102] Some of the plant and
flower motifs recall Jacobean crewel work
but other details are more true-to-life,
particularly the squirrels and birds. Linda
Parry compares this 'naturalistic clarity'
to nineteenth-century Chinese pictorial
embroideries.[103] A pricked and pounced
design for one of the hangings is in the
Ashmolean Museum.[104] The two curtains
are not identical. At the lower edge of the
left hanging, for example, a bird feeds its
chicks hidden in the grass, whereas on the
right, a small bird feasts on a dandelion.

The hangings were offered for sale at
the 1916 exhibition. The price attracted
attention: '"A lady's bedroom", we are
told, "has been furnished by the Women's
Guild of Arts, in which elaboration and
luxury have been purposefully avoided."

Those who read this note would naturally
expect to find that it referred to a bedroom
at a modest cost, but the reverse was the
case...The price of the bedstead alone,
with the hangings, was £170!'[105]

In 1920, the hangings were displayed at
the Detroit Society exhibition of British Arts
and Crafts and purchased by George Booth
(1864–1949), founder of the Cranbrook
Academy, Michigan, whom May met in
Detroit in 1910. Letters in the Cranbrook
Archives reveal that members of the Booth
family visited her in England.[106] Booth was
also an important patron of Morris & Co.,
his support enabling the firm to re-open
the tapestry works after the First World
War.[107] The hangings were used in his own
home until they entered the Cranbrook Art
Museum's collection in 1955.

May kept a photographic record of
her embroideries.[108] In 1923, she thanked
her friend the poet Gordon Bottomley for
a print of these hangings: 'It was really
wonderful of you to take all that trouble
over the photographs of my Detroit
Embroidery...I am delighted, and very glad
to have a record of the work. A thousand
thanks for it. It will be dated, with your
name as photographer on the back, for the
information of the next generation.'[109] **AM**

Bed hangings on display at
the Detroit Society exhibition of
British Arts and Crafts, alongside
Morris & Co.'s tapestry,
David Instructing Solomon, also
purchased by George Booth,
1920

WALLPAPERS AND EMBROIDERY   143

134

Set of four curtains

Designed by May Morris

Embroidered by Elsie Robert, Dorothy
Hardy, Elsie Mochrie, Alice Gimson
and D. K. Kennett, 1916

Wools on hand-woven Italian linen

Worked with darning stitch, long and short
stitch, split stitch, stem stitch, fly stitch,
running stitch and herringbone stitch

178 x 135 (70 x 53 1/8) approx. (each hanging)

National Trust, Wightwick Manor
(NT 1289319.2.1-4) Purchased by
Rosalie Mander from the Kelmscott
Manor sale July 1939, lot 166

Designed for the 1916 Arts and Crafts
exhibition, these curtains were part of
the decorative scheme created by May
and Ernest Gimson and priced at £35.[110]
May favoured the knot motif that also
appears on the Kelmscott Manor bedcover
[see figs 90–92]. One of the curtains was
illustrated in *The Studio Year-Book* and
described as being worked by students
from the Leicester School of Art.[111] Alice
Gimson was a distant relation of Ernest
and the Gimsons were an important
Leicester family.

In 1937, May started corresponding with
Sir Geoffrey and Rosalie Mander, owners
of Wightwick Manor, near Wolverhampton.
The Manders were admirers of William
Morris and keen collectors of Pre-Raphaelite
art. In one letter, May offered these
embroideries for sale: 'The curtains
mentioned above are a set of 4 short
window-curtains. Looking at them afresh
I thought they looked very jolly. I wonder
if you could place them anywhere. I would
let you have them at a very reasonable
price.'[112] A photograph inscribed by May
indicates the price as £60.[113] As it turned
out, the Manders purchased them after
May's death and adapted them as bed
hangings. **AM**

135 and 136
Bedcover
Designed and embroidered by
May Morris, 1910–30
Silks on linen, cotton lining
Worked in stem stitch, satin stitch,
running stitch and French knots
232.4 x 226.1 (91 ¹/₂ x 89)
WMG (F203) Given by Mary Annie
Sloane, 1962

On this coverlet, May successfully employs
knotwork, also seen on William Morris's
bedcover [fig. 90], alternating with sprays of
roses and other hedgerow flowers, berries
and mistletoe. The bedcover is worked in
thick twisted silk, mainly in stem stitch,
with some satin and running stitch and
French knots used for the flowers. The
uncharacteristically bright silk threads
used by May suggest it was stitched
towards the end of her life when a greater
range of synthetically dyed threads was
available. The bedcover design is also in
the William Morris Gallery (A221). **RB**

137

Set of tablemats

Designed and worked by May Morris,

c. 1920s

Wools on canvas, lined with blue linen

Worked in tent stitch

Diameter 17 (6 5/8)

Society of Antiquaries of London:

Kelmscott Manor (KM569.1–8) Given by

Mrs Lucy Winlow (née Constant), 2001

Tablemats like these, worked in petit point or tent stitch, were sold to raise funds for the building of the Morris Memorial Hall at Kelmscott.[114] May exhibited a set of six at the Arts and Crafts exhibition in 1926, priced at £1. 10s. per mat.[115] The Beale family, who lived at Standen, a house designed by Philip Webb in East Grinstead, were among those who purchased them.[116] A notebook with related designs on squared paper survives at Kelmscott Manor. One visitor to Kelmscott in 1925 noted, 'Petit point she despises, but she works at it because of the great demand, making chair seats and table mats and designing them as she goes along.'[117] **AM**

138

Detail from sketchbook

May Morris, c. 1910s–20s

Pencil and watercolour on squared paper

24.8 x 15.3 (9 3/4 x 6) (closed)

Society of Antiquaries of London:

Kelmscott Manor (KM613) Given by Miss Hobbs, 1986

139

Design for a seat cover

May Morris, *c.* 1900–30

Black chalk and bodycolour on paper

68 x 95.3 (26 3/4 x 37 1/2)

V&A (E.960–1954)

May continued to supply Morris & Co. with
designs after 1896 as this design for an
upholstered chair seat demonstrates. Many
other designs and tracings show the extent
to which the company's embroidery work
followed the fashion for the Queen Anne
style in the early twentieth century. This
is probably one of a set of designs for seat
covers, as photographs of two similar
versions are in the archive of the Society of
Antiquaries.[118] May also worked a petit-point
chair seat for Emery Walker, which is still
at 7 Hammersmith Terrace, and is mentioned
in a letter to Walker in 1921.[119] JL

140 and 141
Design or working drawing for a tapestry
May Morris, 1921
Signed 'MM' and dated
Watercolour, pencil and Indian ink
on paper
68.6 x 38.1 (27 x 15)
V&A (E.35–1940) Bequeathed by
May Morris

Tapestry was considered by William Morris to be the highest form of the weaving arts, only attempting to master it himself in later life, and May probably shared this view. On 22 May 1921, she wrote to Emery Walker: 'we are working very hard in house and garden, somehow, though I got 3 hours of tapestry done yesterday and am beginning my figure.'[120] [See also fig. 22.]

The design shows a figure in a loose classical-style gown picking apples or pears in a garden planted with lilies, large red roses and forest flowers in the foreground. A note in the margin reads 'Reduce Roses!'. Marked up with a grid for enlarging onto a cartoon, it is presumably connected with the tapestry panel from a design by Edward Burne-Jones, which May submitted to the 'Exhibition of Decorative Art' at the Royal Academy of Art in 1923.[121] The most likely source is Burne-Jones's painting *Fair Rosamund* of 1863 (Private collection).[122] JL

142 and 143

Bedcover

Designed and embroidered by

May Morris, *c.* 1930

Ivory silk on cotton, silk lining

Worked in chain and satin stitch

203.2 x 160.7 (80 x 63 ¹/₄)

WMG (F202) Given by Mary Annie

Sloane, 1962

For this bedcover May worked in ivory
silk on a white cotton background, using
mainly her favourite chain stitch with
some satin stitch. The overall design
is a geometric network filled with flowers,
wreaths and birds. The two long side
borders are infilled with an acanthus leaf
pattern and the top and bottom borders
with birds and flowers. The bedcover
belonged to Mary Sloane who showed
it under May's name at the exhibition
of Cotswold Craftsmanship, Cheltenham,
in 1951. **RB**

From Miss May Morris, Kelmscott Manor
Lechlade, Gloucestershire

'A Garden Piece' was designed
and worked by me in 1938.
.May. Morris

145

A Garden Piece panel

May Morris, 1938

Silks on linen

Worked in long and short stitch, stem
stitch, satin stitch and French knots

41 x 104 (16 1/8 x 41)

Private collection. Formerly owned
by Percy Horton

This delicate embroidery was worked in
the last months of May's life and shows
that despite deteriorating health she
continued to produce work of the highest
quality. It may be related to an unrealized
commission she received from Sir Geoffrey
and Rosalie Mander for Wightwick Manor.
Perhaps inspired by seeing William Morris's
bed at Kelmscott, the Manders wanted a
valance with an embroidered motto. May
had doubts about the appropriateness
of their scheme; in July 1937 she wrote:
'A Hepplewhite bed, being elegant and
fragile looking, wants furnishing in the
same spirit. You have put in the room
that rich and weighty Acanthus paper
and really I don't think that the bed and
the paper hit it off. The bed itself would
look best with light flowery vallance and
curtains.'[123] This embroidery may be the
trial piece in silks referred to in a letter
dated 7 January 1938.[124] **AM**

ABOVE

144
Detail of May's label on
the reverse.

4

Book Covers and Designs

ANNA MASON

146
Book bag [detail of fig. 161]

THE DESIGNING, PRINTING and binding of books was
a major element of the Arts and Crafts movement. May grew up
in a household where the printed page was treated with an almost
mystical reverence.

As a child, she would have handled the beautiful stamped cloth
bindings designed by Morris and friends, including Dante Gabriel
Rossetti, Philip Webb and Lucy Orrinsmith. As well as access to
her father's library, May was given important volumes of her own,
including a 1633 edition of John Gerard's *Herball*, a fitting exemplar
for a young embroidery designer.[1] She took a keen interest in her
father's experiments in bookmaking, from his early attempts at
calligraphy and illumination, to the famous Kelmscott Press in the
1890s. May's husband, Henry Halliday Sparling, was the first secretary
to the Press [fig. 147]. The extent of her own involvement is unclear
but her name appears on the programmes of annual staff outings
and she saw two volumes through the Press after Morris died.[2]

May designed at least three publishers' bindings. The first, for
an edition of *Irish Minstrelsy*, a collection of songs and lyrics edited
by Sparling, was issued in 1888. May also collaborated with Walter
Crane on a green cloth binding for *Fabian Essays*, edited by George
Bernard Shaw in 1889. The spine of this book is decorated with
delicate leafy stems and hand lettering, which, though attractive in
itself, bears little relation to Crane's socialist iconography on the
cover.[3] More successful was her own binding for *Decorative Needlework*
[see fig. 109]. May was particularly skilled at designing lettering, both
for book covers and the inscriptions that appear in her embroideries.
She also designed the lettering for the stamped bindings of Thomas
J. Cobden-Sanderson, family friend and leading Arts and Crafts
bookbinder.[4]

May's most significant contribution to the book arts was her revival
of the craft of embroidered bindings, an interest she shared with her
mother. In 1883, Jane suggested that Cobden-Sanderson take up
bookbinding, writing: 'That would add an Art to our little community,
and we would work together. I should like to do some little embroideries
for books, and would do so for you.'[5] May herself produced fifteen
known designs for embroidered covers. Over the last decade some of
her bindings have been rediscovered in public collections.[6]

In England the art of embroidered bindings flourished from the
fourteenth century until the mid-seventeenth century. Many precious
books were covered with costly velvets, brocades or silks, embellished
with metal threads and gemstones. Embroidered bags were also made
to protect valuable volumes. When May was creating her first
needlework bindings in the late 1880s, interest in early English
embroidered books was reviving. In 1891, an exhibition of historic
bindings held at the Burlington Fine Arts Club included a case of
embroidered examples.[7] Cyril Davenport, assistant keeper at the British
Museum, published several articles in *The Studio* and a full-length
study in 1899.[8] May visited the British Museum to study historic
bindings at first hand and in *Decorative Needlework* described one that
particularly intrigued her, set with a large flat garnet or ruby.[9]

Most of May's embroidered books were private commissions or gifts.
She enjoyed the opportunity for intricacy afforded by working on a

small scale: 'For small objects on which, owing to their size, much work can be lavished, and which usually need to be enduring and firm, the stiffer forms of couching are particularly suitable. It wears well, and gives scope for greater ingenuity and variety; without which...a small piece of work becomes insignificant, and merely a toy of fashion for the moment.'[10] She worked on the loose covers, the actual binding being done by others, including Cobden-Sanderson and the firms of de Coverly and Zaehnsdorf.

Other Arts and Crafts designers, including Walter Crane, Selwyn Image and Reginald Hallward, also created designs during the short-lived vogue for embroidered bindings. These were usually worked by female embroiderers including Una Taylor, Edith Bloxham and Mary Frances Crane. The Royal School of Art Needlework also exhibited embroidered bindings. Only a few women, such as May, created their own designs.

As well as the elaborate book covers and bags illustrated in this chapter, May also designed simple loose scrapbook or blotter covers that were sold commercially through Morris & Co. [fig. 149]. Worked in thick twisted silk, seven examples are mentioned in the Day Book. A design with roses, wreath and heraldic motifs, illustrated in the Morris & Co. *Embroidery Work* catalogue, c. 1912, might also be attributable to May. AM

ABOVE

148
Design for *Tristan and Isolde* embroidered book cover
May Morris, c. 1890s
Pencil, crayon, ink and watercolour on paper
35 × 49 (13 3/4 × 19 1/4) (paper size)
19.5 × 13.3 × 1 (7 3/4 × 5 1/4 × 3/8) (book size closed)
Ashmolean Museum
(WA1941.108.35), 1941

RIGHT

149
Scrapbook cover
Design attributed to May Morris,
c. 1890s
Silks on linen
Worked in darning stitch,
stem stitch and satin stitch
22 x 28.8 (8 5/8 x 11 3/8)
Private collection

150

Design for *Love Is Enough* front cover
May Morris, 1888
Pencil and ink on paper
30.5 x 21.2 (12 x 8 ³/₈)
Ashmolean Museum (OA1291)

In 1888, May was invited by the bookseller and publisher Frederick Startridge Ellis to design an embroidered cover for a large vellum copy of her father's masque *Love is Enough*. Probably her first embroidered binding, this project is unusually well documented. Ellis devised an unrealized plan for professional and amateur embroiderers to create around 200 covers, to be sold as a collection, dividing the proceeds among the makers.[11] Among those approached was Elizabeth Burden, who for William Morris's version of *The Story of the Volsungs* had embroidered a green velvet cover in gold and coloured silks. 'I should much like to have seen my Aunt's book,' May told Ellis, 'but she has not offered to show it to us.'[12]

The same letter mentions engravings of stamped leather bindings that Ellis had sent May as models for her design. Submitting a sketch of the front cover for approval, May suggested an alternative approach, writing: 'I feel that embroidery work requires [a] different sort of design from the leather-work, as in the latter case one is much restrained by material &

treatment – which restraint gives the work its own peculiar charm. This is the only reason that I proposed making a fresh design, & not by any means mere designer's vanity!'[13]

She continued: 'a very fine thing could be made out of a design to be worked in raised work with gold thread, pearls & garnets on some very good silk velvet, if one could possibly get a piece of finest quality.' The care she lavished on this commission was doubtless linked to her affection for the book; she later recalled listening as a child 'with delight and awakening curiosity to the murmuring of those long swinging lines'.[14]

The design underwent several versions; at one point May considered stitching a couplet from the poem on the back cover.[15] Following the convention of Tudor-era velvet bindings, front and back are treated differently. Displayed loose at the first Arts and Crafts exhibition in 1888, the embroidery was well received: '[It] will no doubt revive the old embroidered book-bindings; for to what better use could one put really delicate work than this?'[16] But it was two more years before May told Ellis, 'Your book cover is finished at last...[it] has grown very dear to me, and yet I am extremely glad it is finished.'[17] Cobden-Sanderson bound the volume in goatskin and attached the cover, finally delivering the work to Ellis in March 1891.[18] **AM**

151

Love Is Enough book cover

Embroidered by May Morris and bound
by T. J. Cobden-Sanderson, *c.* 1888–91

By William Morris, London, 1873

Signed 'M' on lower right of back cover

Gold and coloured silks on silk
with seed pearls

Stitches include long and short stitches,
back stitch, satin stitch, feather stitch,
pistil stitch, French knots, couched gold
and laid work[19]

25.1 x 16.9 x 3.4 (9 7/8 x 6 5/8 x 1 3/8) (closed)

Bancroft Library, University of California,
Berkeley (TYP AA1 A2.A49) Gifted by
Charlotte and Norman Strouse, 1982

152

Design for *Embroidery and Lace*

May Morris, *c.* 1888–91

Pencil and ink on paper

39.2 x 57 (15 ¹/₂ x 22 ¹/₂)

Ashmolean Museum (WA1941.108.32), 1941

153

Embroidery and Lace book cover

May Morris, *c.* 1888–91

By Ernest Lefébure, translated

by Alan S. Cole, London, 1888

Initialled 'M' on the spine

Green silk, embroidered with coloured

silks, gold thread and seed pearls

Worked in split stitch, satin stitch,

long and short stitch, trellis, French

knots and couched gold work

20.5 x 14.2 x 3.1 (8 x 5 ⁵/₈ x 1 ¹/₄)

The Grolier Club of New York (\57.72\vol83)

Formerly collection of Samuel Putnam Avery,

given by E. G. Kennedy, 1930

The subject of this volume, a history of embroidery and lace from antiquity onwards, would have appealed to May. A copy is recorded in William Morris's library and May knew the translator Alan S. Cole, a fellow contributor to Arts & Crafts Exhibition Society catalogues. This is one of May's most successful bindings; the delicate stems grow out of the spine and wrap around the covers of the book. The initials of author and translator appear on the cover and May has signed the spine with a small 'm'. The book is recorded as early as 1891 in the New York collection of Samuel Putnam Avery,[20] art dealer, collector and one of the founders of the Metropolitan Museum of Art. He exhibited the binding at the Grolier Club in 1903.[21] **AM**

154

Design for *The Roots of the Mountains* embroidered book cover

May Morris, *c.* 1889–90

Pencil and ink on paper

28.3 x 52 (11 $^{1}/_{8}$ x 20 $^{1}/_{2}$) (paper size)

20.7 x 17.3 x 3.6 (8 $^{1}/_{8}$ x 6 $^{3}/_{4}$ x 1 $^{3}/_{8}$) (book size closed)

Ashmolean Museum (WA1941.108.33), 1941

William Morris's romance *The Roots of the Mountains*, first published by Reeves and Turner in 1889 and printed by the Chiswick Press, was one of the experimental volumes produced shortly before the founding of the Kelmscott Press. A special issue of 250 copies printed on Whatman paper was bound in Morris & Co. fabric. The ordinary issue of similar dimensions corresponds to the size of May's design. On the left in pencil, she experimented with ways of laying out the monogram 'rHw'.[22] The initials are those of Robert William Hudson (1856–1938); he and his wife, Gerda, were clients of Morris & Co. and friends of the family.[23] The book was published while Jane Morris was spending a month in Wales with the Hudsons and this binding may have been ordered or created as a gift around this time. **AM**

155

Design for *Water Babies* embroidered
book cover

May Morris, *c.* 1890–91

Pencil on tracing paper

28.1 x 41.5 (11 x 16 3/8) (paper size)

19.1 x 12.7 x 3.2 (7 1/2 x 5 x 1 1/4)

(book size closed)

Ashmolean Museum (WA1941.108.31), 1941

In 1891, the booksellers James and Mary Lee Tregaskis organized an exhibition of modern bookbindings by the 'chief European craftsmen'. A total of forty-one copies of Charles Kingsley's *Water Babies*, illustrated by Linley Sambourne, were distributed to binders of repute to cover as they wished. May exhibited two embroidered bindings, one designed by Selwyn Image and this design of her own.[24] The author's initials are worked into the scrolling foliage on the spine. May did not think highly of the book, telling F. S. Ellis, 'I am just now doing a cover for Linley Sambourne's Water Babies of all incongruous things! I am afraid it is growing rather too lavish for so uninteresting a piece of printing.'[25] The book cover is untraced but the catalogue describes May's design as worked in gold and coloured silks on green shot silk. It was one of the most expensive in the exhibition, priced at £13. 13s.[26] **AM**

156

Design for *Omar Khayyam* embroidered
book cover

May Morris, *c.* 1890

Pencil on tracing paper

29.5 x 47.2 (11 5/8 x 18 5/8) (paper size)

18 x 13 x 2.2 (7 x 5 1/8 x 7/8) (book size closed)

Ashmolean Museum (WA1941.108.27), 1941

Unimpressed with Sambourne's
illustrated edition of the *Water Babies*,
May wrote to Ellis, 'I am going to console
myself afterwards, by working a cover for
Omar Khayyam which will be a labour
of love in itself, & which I intend for my
Mother's birthday.'[27] Edward Fitzgerald's
version of the *Rubaiyat of Omar Khayyam*
was popular with the Morris circle. Morris
himself wrote out and illuminated four
versions (some incomplete) in the early
1870s. May's design of scrolling vine
leaves and grapes alludes to the
significance of wine in the poem. The
book cover remained in the family and
was described in the Kelmscott Manor
sale catalogue as embroidered on green
silk. It was purchased by May's relative,
Dr Una Fielding.[28] **AM**

157

Design for *A Study of Dante* embroidered
book cover
May Morris, *c*. 1890
Pencil and ink on paper
30.5 x 50.6 (12 x 20)
20.2 x 14 x 5 (8 x 5½ x 2) (book size closed)
Ashmolean Museum (OA1281), 1941

A Study of Dante by the American educator
Susan E. Blow was first published by G. P.
Putnam & Sons in 1886. A review in the
British Bookmaker confirms that an untraced
embroidered cover based on this design
was exhibited by a Mrs Cave at the 1890
Arts and Crafts exhibition.[29] A pricked
version of the design on tracing paper is
also in the Ashmolean Museum.[30] As with
Love Is Enough, May devised different
treatments for the front and back covers.
The front depicts a rose, surrounded by
flames enclosed within a cartouche. **AM**

158

The Tale of King Florus and the Fair Jehane
Embroidered cover by May Morris,
after 1893
Silks and gold thread on Morris & Co.
St James silk damask
Worked in long and short stitch,
split stitch, satin stitch and French knots
with couched goldwork
15.4 x 11 x 1.7 (6 x 4 3/8 x 5/8)
(book size closed)
The John Rylands Library, The University
of Manchester (R174622) Purchased 2005

This thirteenth-century French romance
translated by William Morris was published
by the Kelmscott Press in 1893. The design
depicts a pair of birds beneath a tree with fig
or vine-shaped leaves.[31] The four tarnished
roundels at the corners of the cover were
once vibrant raised gold work. In 1894,
James and Mary Lee Tregaskis organized
a second popular exhibition of modern
bookbindings, showing seventy-three copies
of this title in unique bindings, although
May was not among the exhibitors.[32] A loose
note inserted in this volume signed by
Bertha Oppenheimer claims that the book
was originally presented to the family of
Hugh Francis Fox by William Morris.[33] **AM**

159
Design for *Schubert Songs* embroidered
book cover
May Morris, undated
Pencil on tracing paper
34.2 x 45.1 (13 $\frac{1}{2}$ x 17 $\frac{3}{4}$) (paper size)
27.3 x 19.3 x 2.1 (10 $\frac{3}{4}$ x 7 $\frac{5}{8}$ x $\frac{7}{8}$)
(book size closed)
Ashmolean Museum (WA1941.108.28), 1941

This attractive design features two pairs
of birds, appropriate for a musical volume.
The monogram has not been identified
with certainty, but may be that of Charles
Harold St John Hornby, founder and
owner of the Ashendene Press.[34] The design
on tracing paper has been pricked and
pounced to transfer the outlines onto
fabric. **AM**

160 and 161

Book bag

Designed by May Morris, embroidered
by May and Jenny Morris, *c.* 1890s
Coloured silks and gold thread on
indigo-dyed linen, lined in pale green silk
Worked in long and short stitch, back stitch,
satin stitch, stem stitch, chain stitch,
loop stitch, buttonhole stitch, laid work
and couching
22.8 x 15.4 (9 x 6)
WMG (F337) Purchased Sotheby's,
23 September 1986, lot 521

This embroidered bag was made for one
of William Morris's medieval manuscripts.
One side is inscribed in Gothic script,
'Psalterium' (book of psalms), and the
other decorated with a stylized pomegranate,
a fitting motif for an ecclesiastical volume
given its traditional association with Christ's
suffering and resurrection. A collaboration
between the two sisters for their father,
the bag remained a treasured family
possession until May's death, being regularly
loaned for exhibitions. In correspondence
May described it as one of her father's
'personal relics'.[35] **AM**

162 and 163

Book bag

Designed and embroidered
by May Morris, 1905–10

Initialled 'M' on the reverse

Coloured silks on blue silk, with glass
beads and pearls

Worked in stem stitch, chain stitch,
long and short stitch, running stitch
and satin stitch

17.8 x 12.7 (7 x 5)

Lisa Unger Baskin Collection, David M.
Rubenstein Rare Book & Manuscript
Library, Duke University (PQ1425.A35
E49 1894), 2015

This bag was designed for a Kelmscott
Press edition of the thirteenth-century
French romance *Of the Friendship of Amis
and Amile*, translated by William Morris
and published in 1894. The book was
bound by May's close friend Katherine
Adams in green morocco leather with
gold tooling and the bag was one of the
embroideries that May exhibited in New
York in 1910.[36] She then gifted the set to
lawyer John Quinn, to whom she inscribed
the volume on 24 March 1910. As the
story is of two friends who refuse to be
separated, this was a telling gift, although
not created especially for Quinn.[37]

May's watercolour design for the
figurative section of the bag is in the
Ashmolean Museum. It is painted to
scale on the back of an invitation card
to the 1905 exhibition held with Katherine
Adams.[38] The bag is a rare example of May
making explicit reference to the narrative
of the book in her design. The two kneeling
figures represent Amis and Amile being
blessed by angels. By their feet are the
identical hanaps or drinking goblets,
presented at their baptism, which enable
them to recognize each other in later life.
This is a superb example of May working
on a minute scale with close attention
to detail – even the plaited silk cord is
embellished with tiny pearls. **AM**

5

Dress and Costume

JENNY LISTER

FASHION AND FEMALE beauty were subjects of great debate in the early 1880s, when May was establishing her career as a designer, embroiderer and teacher. William Morris generally avoided engaging with such issues,[1] although his friends the artists Henry Holiday and Walter Crane actively campaigned for dress reform. However, in 1882 Morris encouraged women not to 'allow yourselves to be upholstered like armchairs, but drape yourselves like women', and argued for freedom of choice and a 'steadiness' in fashion,[2] and in June 1883 he arranged to visit the Rational Dress Association exhibition with May. Morris's textiles, intended mainly for furnishings, were only very rarely used for clothing by his family and friends.[3]

With her unconventional upbringing, dressed in the simple, practical clothes chosen by her mother, and surrounded by her father's experimental textiles, it is unsurprising that May took the matter of dress seriously, developing her own approach. Photographs suggest that she was well aware of the power of clothes to promote her image as an artist and public figure. These images also show the capacity of clothing to demonstrate the Arts and Crafts ideals of truth to materials and simplicity of form.

Several photographs from the late 1880s show May's self-presentation in deliberate interpretations of historic clothing, then regarded as 'Pre-Raphaelite dress'. In one 1886 portrait [see fig. 10] she wears a plain velvet dress, with generously cut sleeves and a natural waistline. With no distracting trimmings, the richness of the velvet contrasts with fine white cuffs, as sometimes seen in Rossetti's paintings of Jane Morris.[4]

One observer recalled May's appearance at the Grosvenor Gallery, which functioned as a kind of Aesthetic fashion show, where 'The dresses were not so very remarkable, except one worn by May Morris, daughter of *The Earthly Paradise*, and she was dressed like the pictures of Raphael. The dark red velvet cap suited her style of beauty, and she was the

observed of all observers, and it was pleasant to look at her.'[5] Fig. 165 shows her wearing such a cap, with an open coat over her dress, reminiscent of Tudor robes. Jeannette Marshall, although she followed the now mainstream fad for Aesthetic dress, was less impressed, describing May wearing a 'brown-red bedgown with no tucker…a guy everyone voted', and later labelling the three Morris women 'witch-like'.[6]

In the early 1890s, May wore trained coats, often with long, open sleeves inspired by Italian Renaissance dress [see figs 9, 11], and enlarged sleeves continued to feature in formal portraits, as in fig. 166 where she wears a long striped open robe, probably of her own invention.

Some garments worn by May could come from the family collection of textiles listed in the Kelmscott Manor sale, which included two Indian saris, two 'eastern Djibbahs', as well as embroidered coats, skirts and dresses reputedly worn by the Morris women.[7] Styles with different cultural and historic traits may also have been designed and worn by May for theatrical projects and costume balls.[8] In 1899,

OPPOSITE

166
May Morris
Photographed by Smedley Aston
Published in *Photography*,
5 November 1904
V&A (401–1905)

she appeared as St Helena of Byzantium in the Art Workers' Guild masque *Beauty's Awakening*,[9] and later she devised costumes for pageants held at Kelmscott.

Picturesque yet functional working dress is seen in images of May at her embroidery frame [see frontispiece and fig. 14]. As well as the comparatively unrestricting sleeves, at least above the elbow, and, now in keeping with general fashion, the dress shown in the frontispiece has an unusual cross-over bodice, and is probably made out of a fine wool or silk mixture. May's dress perhaps bears comparison to the kind of tea gown for 'Work Dress' suggested by Henry Holiday in 1892.[10] A back view of a similar dress reveals that it has a 'Watteau pleat', falling straight to the hem, typical of the Aesthetic garments available from Liberty or Debenhams.[11] Other photographs from the early 1890s [see figs 147, 191] show popular and practical tailored costumes, worn for everyday walking and travel, which are unremarkable apart from a distinctive belt buckle.

Around 1900, high-waisted garments became a distinctive element of May's appearance – the 'perfectly straight down-clinging' dresses described by Bernard Shaw's sister Lucy in 1901,[12] when most women were dressing in closely fitted boned bodices and separate, gored skirts. The effect is demonstrated in a photograph of May, aged about forty, wearing a long dress with a small repeating pattern, a satin neckline bordering the bodice, black lace at the sleeves and long black ribbons [fig. 167].

She designed panels for embroidered bodices suited to this empire-line style, which was also worn by her friends Theodosia Middlemore and Amy Carruthers Tozer [see fig. 171]. These women were ahead of fashion, as a version of the neoclassical style was adopted widely from about 1908, once it was promoted by fashionable couturiers such as Poiret and Lucile. The Morris & Co. *Embroidery Work* catalogue of *c.* 1912 advertised that the company could supply and carry out designs for 'worked yokes or dress panels on customers' own material'.

Surviving photographs, while not representative of May's whole wardrobe, show surprisingly little evidence of her wearing embroidered garments, considering the appreciation of historic embroidered clothing expressed in her writing. Even the dress in the photograph reproduced for the brochure promoting her US lecture tour [see fig. 17] has only a narrow band of embroidery or appliqué edging the low neckline. Frustratingly, no details survive about her lectures 'Historic Dress' and 'Design in Dress', given on that tour, although one report states that perhaps predictably she criticized tight lacing and cheap ready-made clothing, and earnestly argued for natural flowing dress as 'more artistic and much more appealing'.[13] The only garment exhibited in the US was her North African-style cloak [fig. 170].[14] A lecture

on 'Costume and Jewelry', probably for a London audience, was well illustrated with slides including several examples of medieval embroidery, Hans Holbein the Younger's *Ambassadors* (1533), and scenes from a sixteenth-century painted cassone at the V&A.[15]

In the 1910s and 1920s, as hemlines shortened, May sometimes departed considerably from the conventions of fashionable clothing. She evidently found long loose dresses in plain or patterned fabrics, sometimes drawn in at the waist, the most suitable and pleasing for everyday life, and continued wearing them into the 1930s [fig. 168]. Although there are photographs of her in corduroy coat, breeches and long socks at Kelmscott, she was only photographed in such masculine clothing in the privacy of her country garden, or pony trekking in Iceland [see fig. 19]

Sadly no more of May's clothes or dress designs survive, to give further evidence of her attitude to the meaning and value of clothing. While her appearance might have seemed unusual, striking or even odd to some, from a modern perspective May was the consummate practitioner of the art of dress, applying the same thought and expertise to her clothes as she did to her embroidered textiles.

170

Embroidered cape

Designed by May Morris, *c.* 1897

Embroidered by May Morris and

Maude Deacon

Coloured silks on fine wool,

edged with silk braid

Worked in chain stitch, satin stitch

and long and short stitch

123 x 297 (48 ¹/₂ x 117)

WMG (F204) Bequeathed by Mary

Annie Sloane, 1962

In the winter of 1896–97, May visited Egypt with her mother. A photograph [fig.169] shows her wearing an approximation of 'Arabic' dress, presumably on her return, with a cape or cloak similar to the surviving example now at the William Morris Gallery [fig.170]. In the image, May wears a headdress, and around her neck an Egyptian Assuit scarf of black silk embellished with a silver strip. Her underdress may be a Turkish-style robe with open-seamed sleeves.

In the late nineteenth century, 'burnouses' and North African-style capes were fashionable accessories for those who aspired to dress in the Aesthetic style, widely available from Liberty and other shops. May's cape, however, demonstrates her close study of original models, and the application of her artistic and design sense, to create a unique garment, as an example of embroidered dress. It survives in virtually unworn condition, suggesting that the cape was only used for particular occasions and exhibitions, although it would have functioned well as a warm wrapper in the cold months at Kelmscott Manor.

The cape itself is in the form of an abu or abba,[16] a style not particularly associated with Egypt, but worn by Arab men across North Africa and Persia (now Iran). Constructed from two loom widths of fabric, seamed together, both ends were folded in towards the centre and sewn along one edge to form shoulder seams, leaving a horizontal seam around the middle of the garment. Slits were cut for arm holes. Bands of embroidery extend along the shoulder seams and the front closing edges, with an expansive area across the upper back, the design blending North African motifs with May's more characteristic scrolling leaves. The embroidery is mostly chain stitch, with some details worked in satin stitch, single chain stitches and long and short stitch. At least some of the embroidery was worked after the cape was made up, as a design of white stitches disguises the long shoulder seam.

Five related designs are in the Ashmolean Museum. The cape was exhibited in New York in 1910, and in the Women's Guild of Arts room at the 1916 Arts and Crafts exhibition (No. 459). Mary Sloane purchased it from the Kelmscott Manor sale in July 1939, for £2. 17s. JL

169

May Morris in 'Arab-style' dress,

1897

Unknown photographer

WMG (P645) Given by Mrs C.

Bramley, 1962

171

Design or tracing, 'Rough Sketch
for Embroidered Bodice'
May Morris, *c.* 1905
Annotated '18 x 30'
Pencil, with pricking marks on tracing paper
30 x 45 (11³/₄ x 17³/₄)
V&A Archive of Art and Design
(AAD/1990/6)

This tracing paper pattern for the bodice
of a high-waisted dress is rare evidence
of embroidery work relating to a garment
designed by May. The resulting embroidery
would have embellished very high-waisted
dresses similar in profile to those she wore
in the 1900s [see fig. 167]. The design
focuses on a single flower, possibly a
marigold, at the centre front, with scrolling
leaves and smaller stylized flowers
extending up towards the shoulders.
Another tracing at the Ashmolean Museum,
for a panel of embroidery labelled 'Amy
Carruthers' wedding gown' shows that
May designed other embroidered bodices
for her friends. Amy married Henry Tozer
on St Valentine's Day 1908, at St John the
Evangelist in Ladbroke Grove, West London.

Theodosia Middlemore dressed in a
similar way. Her clothing may have been
especially loose because of a medical
condition, but she was described by her
nieces in 1903 as 'tall and imposing, with
short fair curly hair and flowing robes "like
an archbishop's"'.[17] The Day Book shows
that from 1892 to 1896 Morris & Co.
provided only one example of embroidery
for a dress, ordered by Mrs Middlemore,
who in April 1894 paid £3. 12s. for the
design for a 'panel for dress', using her
own silk.[18] JL

Rough Sketch for
Embroidered Bodice.

18 × 30

172 and 173

Dress (bodice and skirt)

Designed and probably embroidered
by May Morris, *c.* 1905

Coloured silks with gold thread on silk,
with metallic machine-made lace

Worked in chain stitch, satin stitch,
stem stitch and long and short stitch

Length 133 (52 3/8) (centre front);
length 147 (57 7/8) (centre back)

Leicestershire Museums (169.1962)[19]

This dress was previously owned by the
artist Mary Sloane, who was May's friend
and a colleague in the Women's Guild
of Arts. While the overall silhouette of
the bodice and skirt is in keeping with
conventional styles, the details of the
layered sleeves, the deep 'V' insert and
the intricate embroidery on the bodice
and at the skirt hem are elements of May's
approach to artistic dress. The embroidery
is worked in outline in chain stitch, with
floral details in satin, stem and long and
short stitches. It may have been made
for a particular occasion, possibly a
masque such as those created by the
Art Workers' Guild.

There is no conclusive evidence to
confirm whether the dress was ever worn
by either May Morris or Mary Sloane, and
it is possible that it is the same 'white
embroidered dress executed by Mrs
William Morris and May Morris' shown
at the Women's Guild of Arts room at the
1916 Arts and Crafts exhibition. A 'white
silk embroidered dress, belonging to Miss
Morris' also appears in the catalogue for
the Kelmscott Manor sale in 1939.[20] JL

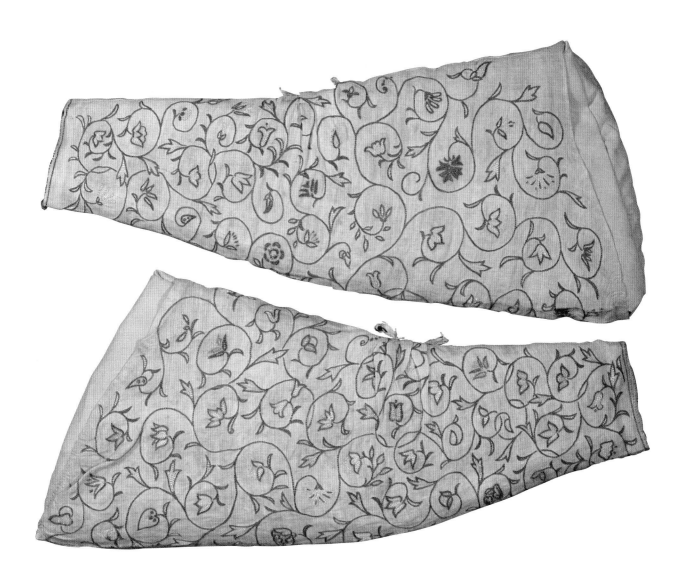

174

Embroidered sleeves

Designed and embroidered

by May Morris, *c.* 1890

Coloured silks on linen

Worked in chain stitch

62 x 29 (24 3/8 x 11 3/8) (each)

National Trust, Wightwick Manor

(NT 1289314)

The chain-stitch embroidery on these sleeves, with trailing leaves and stems enclosing small stylized flowers, emulates English polychrome silk embroidery of the late sixteenth and early seventeenth centuries. They may have been intended for a bodice that was never fully constructed. Their shape echoes some of the voluminous sleeves of bodices worn by women in late Elizabethan portraits.

The sleeves were bought by the Mander family of Wightwick Manor, Wolverhampton, at the Kelmscott Manor sale. JL

6

Jewellery and Metalwork

HANNE FAURBY

175
Necklace
Designed and made
by May Morris, *c.* 1905
[detail of fig. 187]

PRESENTING A LECTURE on jewellery at the Berkeley Lyceum, New York, in December 1909, May Morris concluded: 'Our inspiration must come through love of the rare qualities of gold and silver, and determination to handle these metals sympathetically and directly, with the aid of the fewest and simplest tools.'[1]

This quote, in line with the reform agenda of the second generation of Arts and Crafts practitioners, demonstrates a concern about the state of jewellery design and production shared by May and her contemporaries. Industrial inventions during the nineteenth century had resulted in a market of cheaper mass-produced jewellery where precious metals were pressed, cut and stamped by machine, reducing production time and overall costs.[2] An early, influential initiative for change was undertaken by C. R. Ashbee, who in 1888 founded the Guild of Handicraft, instructing a new generation of jewellery artisans.[3] Ashbee championed what would be a standard principle for Arts and Crafts jewellery, that design should take precedence over material value. He preferred a dull polish for his silver and mainly used semi-precious stones.[4] This was in opposition to mainstream fashion for diamonds, which had become more plentiful thanks to mining exploitation in South Africa.[5]

Many Arts and Crafts practitioners were women who, like May, expressed their artistic abilities through various media. Jewellery making had now become an accepted craft for women to exercise in Victorian England, yet the means to acquire the requisite skills were limited to the art schools or instruction by male family-members. When May joined the Central School of Arts and Crafts to teach embroidery in 1897, access to such training and workshops would have been available to her. As she entered a new chapter in her life, artistically freed from the defined 'Morris style' of Morris & Co., the appeal of jewellery-making must be considered as an opportunity for May to extend her artistic talent in a field not mastered by her father.

The relative ease with which a small jewellery workshop could be set up at home was of equal importance for its accessibility (both practical and cultural) for women.[6] In 1895, *The Studio* magazine illustrated this in an article on the artists Nelson and Edith Dawson who worked from their Chelsea home, where Edith had her enamelling workshop on the first floor.[7]

Other notable Arts and Crafts jewellers were artists Arthur and Georgina (Georgie) Gaskin. In 1899, they presented their first collection, described as a 'Tray of Jewellery', comprising thirteen pieces, at the Arts and Crafts exhibition.[8] A favourable review in *The Studio* noted that their incentive came largely from living in Birmingham, a centre of metalworking and jewellery mass-production. The Gaskins' personal dedication to jewellery reform was also noted as, having other artistic commitments, they used whatever spare time they had in the evenings to see the project through.[9] Being novices in terms of production and technique, their focus was primarily on improved artistic design. Georgie Gaskin was the driving force behind the jewellery production. She did the designs, Arthur the enamels, and the work was executed together with a small team of assistants.[10] The Gaskins were friends of the Morrises, and probably influenced May's own jewellery production.

The exact years in which May produced jewellery are unknown. Her first and last documented displays of jewellery run between the sixth Arts and Crafts exhibition of 1899 and the eleventh exhibition of 1916.[11] For her debut May presented a selection of jewellery consisting of an ecclesiastical gold ring, a sapphire ring, a necklace with pearls and emeralds, a necklace with spinel rubies and eight bead necklaces. These were displayed together with embroideries worked by her and her sister Jenny.[12] This period of May's life was immensely productive. In addition to her creative output she established the Women's Guild of Arts as a professional organization for women equivalent to the all-male Art Workers' Guild.[13]

The jewellery of May Morris is accomplished in execution, subtle and simple in its design – qualities she herself admired in the jewellery of Ancient Greece, which she found 'intimate and tender'.[14] Responding to the hand-beaten fragility of excavated grave ornaments, she brought a less mannered approached to the archaeological style that had been favoured in artistic circles since the Italian jewellers Castellani showed their pieces at London's 1862 International Exhibition.[15] Castellani's copies of ancient jewellery were produced for decades and executed by conventionally trained goldsmiths. Albeit technically sophisticated, compared to the originals May declared their work 'dead as ditch-water'.[16]

May's writings on jewellery reveal her eclectic preferences for historic jewellery and show her engagement with the subject guided as much by the magic and poetry she associated with bygone times as by choice of materials and simple production techniques. Thus, she admired Byzantine regalia [see fig. 181] and portraits of Renaissance women depicted with a sparse number of good quality ornament [see fig. 188]. Referring to the extreme excess of the contemporary fashion for novelties, she singled out jewels of 'pigs done in fine diamonds' and the like as 'most intolerable'.[17]

Her style should be contextualized with an upbringing at the centre of the artistic avant-garde. For, although not a main production focus of the first Arts and Crafts generation, jewellery was integral to the artistic depiction of Pre-Raphaelite women, adding exotic and decorative detail. Photographs of May herself often show her wearing either beaded necklaces [see fig. 16], such as she had worn as a child [see fig. 1], or faint chains with a pendant or brooch. In the portrait of May from 1908 [fig. 176] she wears a ring on each hand, a hair ornament and two necklaces, one of which bears a striking resemblance to a necklace now in the National Museum of Wales [fig. 187]. The chunky beads, most likely a necklace artistically twirled around her arm, contrast with the other delicate pieces she wears and show her ability to put together and play with different styles of jewellery. The, by all accounts, striking and effective ensemble she wore for her jewellery lecture in New York in 1909 further demonstrates her aptitude for combining pieces for effect. The press recorded 'Miss Morris herself wore a heavy dog collar of silver baubles, a large glittering brooch of many varied stones set in silver and a chain of silver, with a heavy blue enamel pendant.'[18]

On May's death much of her estate passed in trust to her companion Mary Lobb, whose death in 1939 effected the final dispersion of Morris family possessions. The auction in July that year included a section devoted to jewellery covering 76 lots, which can be broken down into a minimum of 246 individual pieces.[19] These included rings, pendants, brooches, chains, bracelets and necklaces, watches, snuff boxes, buttons, medals, coins, decorative boxes, fans, beads, scent bottles and a scent purse. Of particular interest here are the boxes of beads and the 'Collection of cut and uncut stones including onyx, shell rosettes, sapphire, turquoise, opals, seed pearls etc' and 'Gold wire, gold solder and gold plates' – all raw materials, survivals of May's workshop and testimony of her years of jewellery production.

177

Necklace

Designed and made by May Morris,

c. 1900

Glass, coral and faience (amulet)

Length 112 (44 ¹/₈)

Manchester School of Art Collection,

Manchester Metropolitan University

Special Collections (MANMU:1902.19),

1902

At the Arts and Crafts exhibition in 1899, May displayed eight bead necklaces.[20] One review noted that 'Miss May Morris, besides her lovely embroideries, shows a rather original set of bead necklaces etc; which prove what excellent effects can be got out of the simplest materials.'[21] This necklace of green glass and coral includes a small Egyptian amulet. According to the original accession register the beads are of Venetian glass. In a letter to Sydney Cockerell on 21 March 1900, May asked him to bring her 'some queer Egyptian beads, amulets [etc.]' from Egypt, as she used such beads 'a great deal' in her necklaces and found they were getting 'scarce and dear in London'.[22] Among items listed in the Kelmscott Manor sale were 'Various boxes of Egyptian beads'.[23] **HF**

178
Necklace
Designed and made by May Morris,
c. 1904
Gold, sapphires, pyrope garnet (front),
almandine garnet (clasp) and seed pearls
Length 37 (14 1/2)
WMG (L18) Given by Marie Lyndon Lang,
1954

This short necklace consists of four
gemstones set in closed-back settings
over heavily tinted foils enhancing their
colour and reflectivity. May will have set
these stones and the pearls herself but
is unlikely to have made the chain.[24]
The necklace was given to Marie Lyndon
Lang by May for her 21st birthday in 1904.
Her father, the ophthalmic surgeon William
Lang, had befriended William Morris in
his youth and purchased Kelmscott Press
books as they emerged.[25] Marie Lyndon
Lang donated this necklace with several
other items, including a *Flowerpot*
embroidery, to the William Morris Gallery
in 1954. **HF**

179 and 180

Ring

Designed and made by May Morris,

c. 1903

Gold and cabochon spinel

2 x 1.9 x 0.5 ($^3/_4$ x $^3/_4$ x $^1/_4$)

V&A (M.19A–1939) Given by Mary Lobb

The smooth and dome-shaped surface treatment of this semi-precious stone is known as cabochon. The spinel is set into a gold ring with a simple but effective acanthus design. The acanthus motif was often used by William Morris and also included in embroidery designs by May. A ring matching this description was exhibited at the Willow Brook Company in New York in 1910.[26]

May advocated using gold with a high carat content in order to retain the metal's original surface. Lower carat gold, she argued, needed greater heat to shape it than the superior, more malleable, quality. As a result the lower carat gold needed to be 'violently polished' and coloured to 'get the fire out of it'.[27] **HF**

181

Pin

Designed and made by May Morris,
c. 1903
Gold, agate, freshwater pearls and emeralds
7.9 x 1.9 x 0.5 (3 $\frac{1}{8}$ x $\frac{3}{4}$ x $\frac{1}{4}$)
V&A (M.20–1939) Given by Mary Lobb

Like other Arts and Crafts jewellery
artisans, May found beauty in irregularly
shaped and coloured stones and would
have thought the speckled qualities of
agate, as seen in this delicate gold pin,
attractive. The emerald drops suspended
by gold chains are strikingly original,
reflecting the way May's interest in drama,
literature and myth influenced her
engagement with jewellery and materials.
When lecturing in America she indulged in
the theatricality of 'the solemn splendour
of a Byzantine crown, with the poetry of
dimly shining emeralds swaying on chains
of gold'.[28] It is likely this pin was exhibited
in 1910 at the Willow Brook Company in
New York.[29] **HF**

183

Pendant

Designed and made by May Morris,

c. 1903

Silver, amazonite, williamsite, seed pearls
and lapis lazuli

5.1 x 2.2 x 0.5 (2 x 7/8 x 1/4)

V&A (M.24–1939) Given by Mary Lobb

This heart-shaped silver pendant suspended
from an open-back set cabochon amazonite
consists of two stylized flowers and a
heart-shaped cabochon williamsite with
inclusions in closed-back setting. Suspended
from the heart are two loops of silver-wired
seed pearls and a drop-shaped, blue and
white lapis lazuli.

The source of inspiration for the pendant
is likely to be a heart-shaped brooch that
was probably given by Rossetti to May's
mother, Jane [fig. 182].[30] He often used
striking jewels as accessories in paintings,[31]
and this brooch is seen in *The Blue Bower*
(1865),[32] as a pendant necklace. Rossetti's
brooch is set with coloured pastes; two
red following the curved shape of the
heart and one green below. It also includes
small stylized flower heads and foliage
similar to those in May's pendant. The
brooch was bequeathed to the V&A by
May together with other jewellery that had
belonged to her mother. The pendant
followed shortly after, gifted to the V&A
in 1939 by Mary Lobb.

The heart-shaped motif was employed
by May in other pieces of jewellery, for
example on the central disk of a girdle
at the V&A [fig. 185] and in the gold
clasps on a necklace now in the National
Museum of Wales [fig. 187]. The former
also includes williamsites, a gemstone
discovered in America in the nineteenth
century, whose green colour offered
a cheaper substitute for jade.

It is evident that May frequently took
inspiration from nature for her jewellery
designs as she did for her embroideries.
Her observations in *Decorative Needlework*
on embroidery design and the role of the
designer may help to contextualize her
approach to jewellery. Constant and
faithful study of nature should be made
in order to intimately understand its
changing appearance. Nature ought to
be re-presented, translated but not copied;
'the living flower should inspire a living
ornament in [the designer's] brain, certain
characteristics being dwelt upon, but the
forms all simplified'.[33]

Heart-shaped designs are seen in
traditional jewellery from Europe and
Scandinavia, popularized in the period
through international exhibitions that
promoted folk culture, dress and
artefacts.[34] The motif was also used
by other Arts and Crafts jewellers such
as Georgie and Arthur Gaskin.[35] **HF**

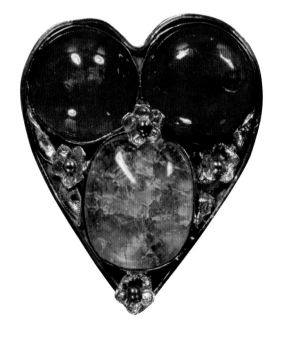

182

Brooch belonging to Jane Morris
V&A (M.40–1939) Bequeathed
by May Morris

184

Brooch

Designed and made by May Morris,

c. 1903–16

Gold, almandine garnets, emeralds,

water opal

3.6 x 3.6 x 1 (1 3/8 x 1 3/8 x 3/8)

William Morris Society (J01) Given by

Dorothy Garratt (née Steele)

The colourful cabochons of this brooch
are in a backless setting, allowing light to
better reflect the vivid gemstones. A fine
twisted gold band runs round the central
opal and the four drop-shaped garnets,
a decorative feature that is also applied on
the silver girdle [fig. 185]. The emeralds,
framed by thick circular gold settings,
close to the centre, give the piece its
balance. The brooch was a gift from May
to Caroline Priscilla Steele, wife of the
medieval scholar Robert Reynolds Steele,
who became May's executor. **HF**

185

Girdle

Designed and made by May Morris,

c. 1905

Silver, williamsite, garnets and

freshwater pearls

Length 71.1 (28); buckle 5.1 x 0.8 (2 x 3/8)

V&A (M.17–1939) Given by Mary Lobb

Displayed at the Arts and Crafts exhibition
in 1906, this silver girdle was priced at
£15.[36] Entitled 'Buckle and Chain' it was
illustrated in *The Studio* magazine.[37] Like
the pendant [fig. 183], the girdle disk is
decorated with small floral motifs and the
three silver chains of the girdle are attached
at intervals to smaller silver disks, each
embossed with a stylized flower head.

Waist ornaments and girdles were worn
in Arts and Crafts circles, a historicist
fashion connoting both medieval and
Renaissance modes of embellishment.
A seventeenth-century German marriage
belt bequeathed to the V&A by May
(M.34–1939) is seen in Rossetti's painting
Astarte Syriaca (1877).[38] Photographs show
May wearing waist ornaments [see fig. 191]
and two girdles were listed in the
Kelmscott auction catalogue.[39] **HF**

186

Hair ornament

Designed and made by May Morris,

c. 1905

Silver, pearls, opals and garnets

14.7 x 3.1 x 14.8 (5 3/4 x 1 1/4 x 5 3/4)

National Museum of Wales

(NMW A 50696) Given by Mary Lobb

This hair ornament takes the shape of
a wreath with foliage and berries, thus
combining both nature and the ancient
world – two of May's main sources of
inspiration. In using opals May challenged
the popular perception that they were
unlucky,[40] writing in their defence: 'The
fragile opal...is sympathetic and sensitive
to change. The idea of connecting this
stone with misfortune is quite modern,
for of old days it was reputed to embody
all the virtues of all other stones, in so far
as it contained their manifold colours.'[41] **HF**

187
Necklace
Designed and made by May Morris,
c. 1905
Gold and garnets
Length of chain 38.6 (15 1/4);
length of leaf from chain 3.6 (1 3/8);
maximum width 12.6 (5)
National Museum of Wales
(NMW A 50697) Given by Mary Lobb

The inspiration for this necklace may have
been the fine gold jewellery found in
tomb-excavations. May certainly delighted
in the 'thin slips of gold beaten and
twisted into objects that may be needed
for solace or use in the dim life beyond the
threshold'.[42] In its delicate design, with
crumbled, shaped leaves, this necklace
evokes the simple, effective techniques
applied in ancient funerary ornaments.[43]
The handmade and unique qualities of the
piece effectively contrasts it to commercial
work of this type. The necklace was
displayed at the Arts and Crafts exhibition
in 1916, priced at £10.[44] **HF**

188

Sleeve clasps

Designed and made by May Morris,

c. 1905

Silver, garnets, chrysoprase and agate

5 x 3.9 x 0.8 (2 x 1 ¹/₂ x ³/₈)

National Museum of Wales

(NMW A 50699-700) Given by Mary Lobb

May's lectures in America in 1909–10 prompted a display of her work in New York. A pair of 'sleeve ornaments' were included, probably those illustrated here.[45] An article entitled 'Vulgar Jewelry – Miss May Morris Talks on Tendency to Sheer Display', quoted her admiration for Holbein's portraits of women with jewelled sleeves, and her wish 'that modern women would adopt the style'.[46] Such sleeves were gathered at intervals by a jewel allowing the chemise sleeve underneath to be pulled through the gaps.[47] **HF**

189

Spoon

Designed and made by May Morris,

c. 1899–1906

Silver, garnet

12.3 x 2.8 (4 $^7/_8$ x 1 $^1/_8$)

National Museum of Wales

(NMW A 50287) Given by Mary Lobb

May did not limit her metalwork production to jewellery alone. Two silver spoons made by her are held by the National Museum of Wales, of which one is illustrated here. It has been identified as the 'Baby's spoon' exhibited in the Willow Brook Company rooms in New York in 1910.[48] The tip of the handle ends with a garnet in a closed-back setting. The bowl of the spoon is cupped by a thin tongue joining bowl and handle. This technique provides strength to the spoon and is reminiscent of the tongues seen on antique rat-tail spoons; a likely source of inspiration for May. 'Three Charles II rat tail table spoons' are included in the Kelmscott auction catalogue.[49] **HF**

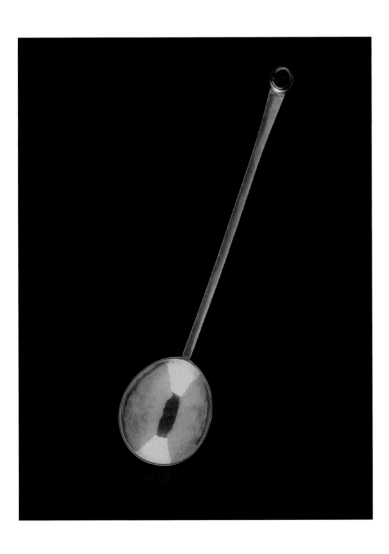

Waist buckle.
The leaves and tendrils of beaten silver
laid on a silver plate; the latter covered
with a punched diaper

190

Design for waist buckle

May Morris, c. 1897–1907

Ink and pencil on paper

11.6 x 17.5 (4 1/2 x 6 7/8)

Ashmolean Museum (WA 1941.108.2), 1941

By the 1880s, a fashion for waist ornaments, either converted directly from, or in the shape of, antique Dutch book clasps had become fashionable in artistic circles.[50] The brace-like outline of this buckle suggests inspiration taken from such clasps, though without the central element that, as a book clasp, would have covered the back of the book. Instead the two brace-shaped plates are joined together by a pin entwined by vine tendrils. In fig. 191 May wears a waist ornament of this type. Meanwhile the vine leaf design shares strong similarities with the *Vine Leaf* table cover [see fig. 97] designed by May around 1896. The design is inscribed: 'Waist buckle. The leaves and tendrils of beaten silver laid on a silver plate, the latter covered with a punched diaper.' **HF**

191

Left to right: May Morris,
Henry Halliday Sparling, Anna
Oscara Steffen (née Von Sydon),
Gustaf Steffen
Unknown photographer
Bromide print, c. 1892–93
7 x 8.9 (2 ⅞ x 3 ½)
National Portrait Gallery
(NPG x32598) Given by
Robert R. Steele, 1939

NOTES

Bibliographical references given in abbreviated form in the Notes are given in full in the Sources and Further Reading.

ABBREVIATIONS
ACES Arts & Crafts Exhibition Society catalogues, by year of exhibition
MM May Morris
WMG William Morris Gallery
WMS William Morris Society

FOREWORD PP. 6–7

1   Lockwood and Glaister 1878, p. 8.
2   Sedding 1893, p. 406.
3   Glaister 1880, p. 26.
4   May Morris, 'Embroidery', in Mackmurdo 1892, p. 46.

1. A WELL-CRAFTED LIFE PP. 8–31

1   MM, 'Journal of My Visit to Naworth Castle', 1870. WMG (J2416)
2   Morris 1973, 1, pp. 306, 370, 378.
3   MM to G. B. Shaw, 5 May 1886, British Library Add. MS 50541.
4   Crane 1905, p. 22.
5   Morris 1936, 1, p. 7.
6   Morris 1893, pp. 105–6.
7   MM in Gordon 1900.
8   Parry 1996, p. 62.
9   Morris 1893, pp. 108–9.
10   May Morris, draft address to WGA, WMS collection.
11   MM to J. Quinn, 6 December 1910, Londraville 1997, pp. 68–69.
12   Ibid., p. 70.
13   See Paris 1914.
14   MM to J. Quinn, 31 December 1915, Londraville 1997, p. 167.
15   MM to J. Quinn, 5 December 1915, Londraville 1997, p. 157.
16   MM to James Leatham, 25 November 1926, University of Aberdeen MS 2776/18/4.
17   MM to James Leatham, 13 June 1931, University of Aberdeen MS 2776/18/5.
18   Manning 1980.
19   Fielding 1968.
20   MM to G. B. Shaw, 5 May 1936, Harry Ransom Center, University of Texas at Austin.
21   M. F. V. Lobb to Eric Maclagan, V&A, quoted Parry 1996, p. 59.

2. SKETCHES AND WATERCOLOURS PP. 32–55

1   D. G. Rossetti to Jane Morris, 10 March 1880, letter 108, Bryson and Troxell 1976, p. 149.
2   Delaware Art Museum 2010 (1936-26).
3   Morris 1973, p. 106.
4   Ibid., p. 230.
5   See Dickens 1879, p. 10, and Sparkes 1884, p. 108.
6   See Marsh 1986, p. 160.
7   Poynter 1880, p. 106.
8   Hobbs & Chambers 1939.
9   Morris 1973, p. 338.
10   William Morris to Jenny Morris, December 1877, Kelvin 1996, vol. 1, p. 418.
11   Kelmscott Manor Collection.
12   Morris 1973, p. 377.

13   Ibid., p. 336.
14   Weintraub 1986, 1, p. 146.
15   May Morris to Bernard Shaw, 16 February 1886, British Library Add. MS 50541, f.62.
16   Weintraub 1986, 1, 12 September 1886, p. 197, 1 January 1887, p. 230, 15 November 1892, p. 872.
17   Shaw, 'Morris as I Knew Him', Morris 1936, 2, p. xxvii. See also MM annotated proofs, British Library Add. MS 50665, f.279.
18   Jonsdottir 1986, p. 19.

3. WALLPAPERS AND EMBROIDERY PP. 56–151

1   MM studied here for a few years, according to the pamphlet advertising her American speaking tour, 1909–10. WMG J910.
2   'Our Ladies' Column', *The Preston Chronicle and Lancashire Advertiser*, 14 October 1893, p. 7. This article is available on the British Newspaper Archive: www.britishnewspaperarchive.co.uk
3   See White 2017.
4   Ada Nield Chew, 1894, quoted in Rowbotham 2010.
5   National Archives Currency Converter 1890–2005: www.nationalarchives.gov.uk/currency
6   Harvey and Press, p. 197.
7   A newspaper article in the *Morning Post* on 12 May 1891, p. 3, specifically comments on this piece in an exhibition of embroidery by the Royal School of Art Needlework: 'The most striking piece of tapestry executed in the school is a fine wall-hanging, designed by Mr Burne-Jones and Mr William Morris, and arranged and worked under the direction of Miss May Morris and Miss Barker. The picture consists of an ideal representation of Pomona holding a spray of apple blossom in her hand, and the execution of it has occupied three ladies of the school regularly for 10 months.' (Note: embroidery was often referred to as 'tapestry' in this period). British Newspaper Archive: www.britishnewspaperarchive.co.uk
8   *Woman's World*, 1890, p. 122.
9   Morris 1936, 1, pp. 39–44.
10   V&A Archive, Nominal file MA/1/M2833.
11   Paris 1914, no. 514. The catalogue entry states that the coverlet was worked by May Morris and her pupils.
12   A hanging described as *Acanthus*, probably designed by Dearle, is in the Art Gallery of South Australia (Menz 1994, no. 53).
13   V&A (1133–1875) and (1134–1875).
14   At least three versions of *Flowerpot* are recorded in the Day Book. A partially worked kit cost 14s., or 5s. to have the design traced onto the customer's own fabric.
15   ACES 1890, no. 199; Willow Brook 1910, no. 6.
16   *Centenary of William Morris: Catalogue of Exhibition 1934*, London, 1934, p. 18, no. 65.
17   *Embroidery Work*, c. 1912, Morris & Co.
18   Dreweatts, Donnington Priory: *Interiors – to include selected items from the Collection of Laurence W. Hodson (1863–1933)*, 27 February 2013, lot 78.
19   Order no. 1502, February 1893.
20   Traced design on paper in AAD/1990/6 file 1, and T.61-1976.
21   Morris 1893, p. 30.
22   Illustrated in Godwin 2015.
23   Hobbs & Chambers 1939, part of lot 171.
24   Morris 1888, p. 29.
25   Morris 1893, pp. 14–15.
26   Menz 1994, p. 96.
27   Day Book, order no. 1816, 14 September 1894.
28   The acquisition of the designs and tracings appears to have been negotiated from Morris & Co. via May Morris, although the precise sequence of events is obscure. See V&A Archive, Nominal file MA/1/

M2833: MM to Kendrick, V&A curator, 23 February 1919: '[Morris & Co.] have piles of designs, and mounted...but they really ought to be considered as museum things now, – this entre nous please.'

29   *A Study and Catalog of Morris & Co Designs in the Collection of the William Morris Center [sic]*, London, George Monk and Walter Gooch, 1978, ref. C.44.

30   Also known as 'Orchard', see Morris 1962, fig. 52, p. 110.

31   *The World*, 3 October 1888, cited Marsh 1986, p. 220.

32   Morris 1890, p. 95.

33   For a photograph, *c*. 1909, and extended discussion, see Carlano 1993, fig. 2, p. 19.

34   AAD/1996/6 file 1-4.

35   *Embroidery Work*, *c*. 1912, Morris & Co.

36   Day Book, order no. 1544, 4 April 1893.

37   Paris 1914, no. 530, *La Verger*, or 'The Orchard', p. 65.

38   'Victorian and Edwardian Decorative Arts', V&A, 1952.

39   No. 1634, 13 September 1893.

40   Menz 1994, no. 158, ill. p. 51.

41   Fine Costume and Textiles, Christie's South Kensington, 19 November 1991, lot 189.

42   Fine Twentieth Century Design, Sotheby's, 28 April 2009, lot 4.

43   V&A (10–1961).

44   Julia Dudkiewicz, 'Memorialising her father's legacy: May Morris as curator and gatekeeper of William Morris's estate and the role of Kelmscott', in Hulse 2017. The author is grateful to Julia Dudkiewicz for generously sharing her research for this and her PhD (Central Saint Martins, University of the Arts London) on Kelmscott Manor. Linda Parry also very kindly gave her opinion on the dating of the bedcover.

45   Christie's King Street, 1 May 2013, lot 34.

46   Including an inlaid chest designed by George Jack, V&A (Circ.40–1953).

47   Morris 1936, 1, p. 59.

48   Carruthers 2013, pp. 201–26.

49   Annette Carruthers' essay in Hulse 2017 and Claire Maugueret, Lore Troalen, Stephen Jackson and Alison N. Hume, 'Dye Sources used by May Morris in the embroideries from Melsetter House', poster presented at the Dyes in History and Archaeology conference, Pisa, October 2016.

50   Morris 1893, p. 29.

51   Dreweatts, Donnington Priory: *Interiors – to include selected items from the Collection of Laurence W. Hodson (1863–1933)*, 27 February 2013, p. 23.

52   See Faurby and Lister, in Hulse 2017.

53   ACES 1906, pp. 65–66, no. 243 (g & i); *The Studio*, 37:157 (April 1906), p. 221.

54   Parry 1996 [2], cat.M22, V&A (T.192–1953).

55   The slightly larger measurements given in the 1896 note will include the borders of the panels, now hidden by the frames of the folding screen.

56   See for example, cat. nos 36, 37 and 43 in Browne, Davies, Michael and Zöschg 2016.

57   Manning 1980, pp. 18–19.

58   ACES 1890, p. 173, no. 204. 'The Arts and Crafts Exhibition', *Illustrated London News*, 11 October 1890, p. 454.

59   Willow Brook 1910, no. 1.

60   Haslam 2016, pp. 3–5.

61   The source and meaning of many of the quotations have been identified by Jill Halliwell; document available to consult at Kelmscott Manor.

62   May owned a photograph of the Girona embroidery, now in the Ashmolean Museum.

63   Typescript of lecture 'Pattern-Designing', WMG, Briggs archive, p. 18.

64   The designs are rolled and too fragile to consult until conservation work is undertaken.

65   Quoted in Haslam 2016, p. 3.

66   MM to Anne Cobden-Sanderson, 11 December 1884, British Library RP5966(vi).

67   Swain 1980, pp. 94–95.

68   The collection at the Ruskin & Morris Center contains lantern slides of four drawings of medieval minstrels with cymbals, portative organ, shawm and psaltery respectively. The Ashmolean design measures 29.7 x 23.5 (11³/₄ x 9¹/₄) (OA1286).

69   V&A (C.677-682–1923).

70   ACES 1893, p. 36, no. 199b. Another 'Music Figure' was exhibited ACES 1916, p. 210, no. 458(w).

71   Morris 1888, p. 25.

72   See Morris 1889, Morris 1890, Mackmurdo 1892 and Morris 1893 [2].

73   Bancroft Library, University of California, Berkeley: MM to unknown recipient, 18 May 1891.

74   Morris 1893, p. 2.

75   Ibid., p. 5; V&A (175–1889).

76   In 1886, William Morris sold a chain-stitch coverlet from Bengal to the South Kensington Museum (V&A: 616–1886). This corresponds to the type of Indian embroidery produced for the European market described in *Decorative Needlework*, pp. 17–18.

77   Morris 1893, p. 64. Resht prayer mat, Birmingham Museum and Art Gallery (1939M26). Our thanks to Rebecca Bridgman, Curator of Islamic & South Asian Arts, for bringing this collection to our attention. A lantern slide of the Resht embroidery was used by MM in her lectures. The slides are owned by the Art Workers' Guild.

78   Morris 1893, p. 79. For discussion of embroidery manuals, see Lynn Hulse's introductory essay in Higgin 2010, pp. 1–36.

79   Morris 1893, p. 84.

80   Ibid., p. 90.

81   Ibid., p. 111.

82   Ibid., p. 30.

83   Quoted in Masterman 1984, p. 167.

84   16ff. in folder marked 'Birmingham No. 2' (J561i-xvi).

85   WMG (J561vii).

86   Botanical study of citrus aurantium, Ashmolean Museum (WA1941.108.48).

87   V&A (W.4–2003). Image at http://anglicanhistory.org/women/rich_deaconesses1907/, accessed 3.10.2016. Our thanks to Kate Hay, Furniture, Textiles and Fashion department, V&A.

88   ACES 1899, p. 47; Willow Brook 1910, cat. no. 16; and Paris 1914, cat. no. 516.

89   OA1300 and OA1294.

90   See Moore 1933.

91   Hoban 2014, p. 189.

92   New Zealand 1906, p. 60. Two versions of this design were worked and are visible in photographs of the New Zealand International Exhibition, Christchurch, 1906–07.

93   Margery Burnham Howe, *Deerfield Embroidery* (New York, Scribner's, 1976). Our thanks to Lynn Hulse for this suggestion.

94   MM to Sydney Cockerell, 26 August 1923, WMG.

95   Morris 1893, p. 81.

96   MM to Sydney Cockerell, 9 September 1923, WMG. See also British Library Add. MS 52740.

97   Sir John Auld Mactaggart (1867–1956) married Elizabeth Ann Orr ('Lena') in 1928. Provenance information comes from the object file at Kelmscott Manor.

98   Mackmurdo 1892, p. 48.

99   ACES 1916, p. 212, no. 458 (ii).

100   For May's collaborations with Gimson see Greensted 2017.

101   'Arts & Crafts: A Review of the Work executed by Students in the leading Art Schools of Great Britain and Ireland', *The Studio* 66:274 (January 1916), p. 13.

102   ACES 1916, p. 214.

103   Parry 2013, p. 41.

104   Ashmolean Museum (WA1941.108.46).

105   'Arts and Crafts at the Royal Academy (Second Article)', *The Studio*, 69:285 (December 1916), pp. 126–28. One hanging was subsequently illustrated in *The Studio: Year-Book of Decorative Art*, 1917, p. 107.

106   Ellen M. Dodington, *Cranbrook and the British Arts & Crafts Movement: George Booth's Legacy*, Cranbrook Art Museum exhibition guide, 2003. May gave two lectures in Detroit: 'Pageantry and the Masque' for the Detroit Society of Arts and Crafts on 19 January 1910 and 'Historical Costumes' for the Women's Indoor Athletic Club on 20 January 1910.

107   See Parry 1983 [2].

108 See V&A (4-38.1961) and Society of Antiquaries (MS 984/4). Some of the photographs are annotated by May on the reverse.

109 MM to Gordon Bottomley, 10 June 1923, British Library Add. MS 88957/1/70 f.143.

110 ACES 1916, p. 212, no. 458(mm).

111 *The Studio: Year-Book of Decorative Art*, 1917, p. 106. A partially coloured design survives in the Ashmolean Museum (WA1941.108.49).

112 MM to Geoffrey Mander, 7 January 1938, Wightwick Manor.

113 MM's inscription: 'One of a set of 4 curtains in wools on hand woven Italian linen. Bright coloured band and yellow knot work. 5ft long x 4'6" wide each. The set of four £60'. Society of Antiquaries (MS 984/4).

114 Breakspear 1983, pp. 13–14.

115 ACES 1926, p. 65, no. 218(n). For photographs inscribed in May's hand see Society of Antiquaries (MS 984/4).

116 Three mats are in the collection at Standen, at least two purchased during the Beales' residency.

117 Manning 1980, p. 19.

118 Society of Antiquaries (MS 984/4).

119 MM to Emery Walker, 18 April 1921, WMG (J507).

120 WMG (J445).

121 *Exhibition of Decorative Art, Winter Exhibition*, Royal Academy of Arts, London, 1923, p. 43, no. 582. Thanks to Anna Mason for this reference.

122 See Julia Dudkiewicz, 'The Kelmscott Manor *Venus* and Morris's idea for a "House of Love" at Red House', *Useful and Beautiful* (William Morris Society in the US), (Winter 2016.1), pp. 3–18 at p. 16. Thanks to Alison Smith for this suggestion.

123 MM to Geoffrey Mander, 15 July 1937, Wightwick Manor.

124 Twelve letters from MM to Geoffrey Mander are at Wightwick Manor, dating between 2 May 1937 and 9 March 1938.

4 . BOOK COVERS AND DESIGNS PP. 152–173

1 Society of Antiquaries of London (Kelmscott Manor) (inscribed 'May Morris with her fathers love March 25th 1882'). In his essay 'Design', John D. Sedding wrote: 'For the unskilled designer there is no training like drawing from an old herbal', Sedding 1893, p. 412.

2 *The Water of the Wondrous Isles* (1897) and *The Sundering Flood* (1898); MM to Sydney Cockerell, 21 January 1913, WMG.

3 For May's publishers' bindings see Masterman 1984, pp. 163–67.

4 MM is credited with designing Cobden-Sanderson's lettering in ACES 1889, p. 124, no. 104 and 1890, p. 150, no. 88.

5 Cobden-Sanderson 1926, 1, p. 94.

6 An embroidered silk cover (12 x 17.5; 4 3/4 x 6 7/8) for a 1919 edition of *News From Nowhere* in the University of St Andrews may also be attributable to MM. The volume was owned by George and Ada Culmer who cared for May's sister, Jenny, until August 1917. MM and Ada remained close and fifteen letters from MM to Ada are in the Lisa Unger Baskin Collection, Duke University, Durham, North Carolina.

7 Duff and Prideaux 1891, pp. 116–22.

8 Davenport 1894, pp. 208–12, and Davenport 1899.

9 MM to F. S. Ellis, 9 May 1888, Bancroft Library, University of California, Berkeley; Morris 1893, pp. 53–54.

10 Morris 1893, pp. 54–55.

11 F. S. Ellis to T. J. Cobden-Sanderson, 2 January 1888, Cobden-Sanderson Papers, Special Collections, Smith College Libraries, Northampton, Massachusetts, quoted Tidcombe 1996, pp. 79–80.

12 MM to F. S. Ellis, 9 May 1888, Bancroft Library, University of California. The book, included in the sale of Miss Vivian Lobb's estate, Hodgson & Co. 1939, p. 36, lot 471, is currently untraced.

13 MM to F. S. Ellis, 9 May 1888, Bancroft Library, University of California, Berkeley.

14 Morris 1973, 1, p. 248.

15 Design for back cover as executed is in the Ashmolean Museum (WA1941.108.26).

16 ACES 1888, p. 125, no. 145; 'The Arts and Crafts Exhibition', *The Nation*, 25 October 1888, p. 331.

17 MM to F.S. Ellis, 7 October 1890, Bancroft Library, University of California.

18 For the binding technique see Tidcombe 1984, pp. 288–89. MM made the cover slightly too small so it was enlarged with a silk flap. A scale drawing, with instructions by Cobden-Sanderson, is in the Ashmolean Museum (WA1941.108.47).

19 It has not been possible to examine the work in person so the description of the stitches is provisional.

20 Du Bois 1892, p. 60; New York 1919, p. 93, lot 546.

21 *Exhibition of Silver, Embroidered and Curious Book-bindings*, Grolier Club, New York, 1903, p. 76, no. 228.

22 A pricked version of the final design on tracing paper is in the Ashmolean Museum (OA1280).

23 Sharp and Marsh 2012, p. 189.

24 A pricked design for the Selwyn Image binding is in the Ashmolean Museum (WA1941.108.29). It was worked on white silk in gold, silver and coloured silk threads.

25 MM to Frederick Ellis, 7 October 1890, Bancroft Library, University of California, Berkeley.

26 *Exhibition of Modern Bookbindings by the Chief European Craftsmen, at the Caxton Head, 232, High Holborn, on Monday March 2nd, till Saturday 14th... Catalogue*, J. & M. L. Tregaskis, Caxton Head, London, 1891, nos 38–39, p. 14.

27 MM to Frederick Ellis, 7 October 1890, Bancroft Library, University of California, Berkeley.

28 Hobbs & Chambers 1939, Mary Annie Sloane annotated version (WMG), lot 168. Many of Dr Fielding's possessions were destroyed during the Second World War and the book cover is not known to have survived.

29 *British Bookmaker*, 4:41 (1890), p. 17. ACES 1890, p. 149, no. 86. Mrs Cave may have been related to architect Walter Cave (1863–1939), a member of the Art Workers' Guild and ACES exhibitor. His wife, Jessica Maria Cochrane, also exhibited at ACES but they were not married until 21 June 1892. A Mrs Cave ordered a 'specially designed' book cover through Morris & Co. in August 1894 (Day Book).

30 Ashmolean Museum (WA1941.108.50).

31 A pricked design for the binding is in the Ashmolean Museum (WA1941.108.34) and a photograph of the embroidery before it was bound is in the V&A (12.1961).

32 See Tidcombe and Middleton 1994.

33 Ramwell 2005/6, p. 11.

34 See Masterman papers, The Women's Library, London School of Economics (7MMO/1/168).

35 Exhibited ACES 1899 and Paris 1914, no. 513. Purchased by Mary Annie Sloane from the Kelmscott Manor sale, 1939, lot 170 (erroneously described as green). See also MM to Emery Walker, 14 September 1919, WMG (J494).

36 Willow Brook 1910, no. 15.

37 For the friendship and brief romance between MM and John Quinn see Londraville 1997.

38 Ashmolean Museum (WA1941.108.42).

5 . DRESS AND COSTUME PP. 174–187

1 See Calvert 2012 for comprehensive discussion of artistic dress 1848–1900.

2 Morris 1882, pp. 174–232.

3 WM to MM, 8 June 1883, Kelvin 1996, 2, p. 98. See Parry 1983, p. 61 and 2nd edition, 2013, p. 73, and MacCarthy 2010, pp. 403 and 445.

4 Such as *The Day Dream* (1880), V&A (CAI.3).

5 Partington 1921, p. 158.

6 Shonfield 1987, pp. 117–18.

7   Hobbs & Chambers 1939.

8   Walter Crane to MM, 10 March 1884, British Library Add. MS 45346, ff.4–5.

9   Programme, *Beauty's Awakening, A Masque of Winter and of Spring*, presented by the members of the Art Workers' Guild, performed in the Guildhall, London, June 1899. With thanks to Monica Grose-Hodge, the Art Workers' Guild.

10 Henry Holiday, 'The Artistic Aspect of Dress', a paper read by Mr Henry Holiday at a meeting of the H & A D U on May 6th, 1892, *Aglaia*, Journal of the Healthy and Artistic Dress Union, I (July 1893), p. 23.

11 See NPG x19855.

12 Lucy Carr Shaw to Janey Crichton, 24 July 1901, quoted Farmer, 1959, p. 140. Quoted Marsh 1986, p. 236.

13 *Spokane Press*, 29 January 1910, p. 5; our thanks to Margaretta Frederick for this reference.

14 Willow Brook 1910, p. iv.

15 Women's Guild of Arts, slides illustrating lecture by Miss May Morris 'Costume and Jewelry', now at the Art Workers' Guild. The cassone mentioned is V&A (4639–1858).

16 Moya Carey, Curator of Middle Eastern Textiles, V&A, suggests that the most likely model is an abu rather than a djibbah. Many thanks, too, to Jennifer Wearden for very helpful comments.

17 Quoted Carruthers 2013, p. 202. See also R. Smith, 'Leaping over Oblivion: A Family Memoir', unpublished typescript , 1993, Chapter 8, note 5.

18 Order no. 1736.

19 Our thanks to Sarah Nicol, Inspiring Collections Officer, Leicestershire County Council for assistance.

20 ACES 1916, no. 459, and Hobbs & Chambers 1939, lot 137.

31 Bury 1991, pp. 469–71.

32 Now Barber Institute of Fine Arts, University of Birmingham.

33 Morris 1893, new edn 2010, p. 40.

34 Gere and Rudoe 2010, p. 328.

35 Bury 1976, p. 102.

36 ACES 1906, p. 126.

37 'The Arts and Crafts Exhibition at the Grafton Gallery. Third and concluding notice', *The Studio*, 157 (April 1906), pp. 213–29 at p. 224.

38 Now Manchester Art Galleries.

39 Hobbs & Chambers 1939.

40 Gere 1975, p. 99.

41 Morris 1909, Jewelry, p. 15.

42 Ibid., p. 8.

43 Phillips 1996, p. 9.

44 Sloan 1989, p. 13; ACES 1916, p. 213.

45 Willow Brook 1910; Sloan 1989, p. 12.

46 'Vulgar Jewelry – Miss May Morris talks on tendency to sheer display', *New York Daily Tribune*, 17 December 1909.

47 Cunnington 1970, p. 63.

48 Sloan 1989, p. 13.

49 Hobbs & Chambers 1939.

50 Gere and Rudoe 2010, pp. 299–301.

6. JEWELLERY AND METALWORK PP. 188–207

1   Morris 1909, Jewelry – Conclusion, p. 4.

2   Phillips 2008, pp. 94–95.

3   'British Decorative Art in 1899, and the Arts and Crafts Exhibition, Part II', *The Studio*, 79 (November 1899), pp. 104–30 at pp. 118–20.

4   Callen 1979, pp. 154–55.

5   Phillips 1996, pp. 150–51.

6   Callen 1979, pp. 154–56.

7   'A chat with Mr. and Mrs. Nelson Dawson on enamelling', *The Studio*, 33, (December 1895), pp. 173–78.

8   ACES 1899, p. 50.

9   'British Decorative Art in 1899, and the Arts and Crafts Exhibition, Part III', *The Studio*, 81 (December 1899), pp. 179–96 at p. 193.

10 Breeze and Wild 1981, pp. 61–62.

11 Sloan 1989, pp. 11–12.

12 ACES 1899, p. 47.

13 Marsh 1986, p. 251.

14 Morris 1909, Jewelry, pp. 6–7.

15 Soros and Walker 2005, pp. 243–45.

16 Morris 1909, Jewelry, p. 2.

17 'Vulgar Jewelry – Miss May Morris talks on tendency to sheer display', *New York Daily Tribune*, 17 December 1909.

18 Ibid.

19 Hobbs & Chambers 1939.

20 ACES 1889, p. 47.

21 *The Warder and Dublin Weekly Mail*, 14 October 1899, p. 6.

22 MM to Sydney Cockerell, 21 March 1900, William Morris Gallery (S4.3.16).

23 Hobbs & Chambers 1939.

24 Sloan 1989, p. 12.

25 Royal College of Surgeons, Plarr's Lives of the Fellows Online: William Lang, http://livesonline.rcseng.ac.uk/biogs/E004333b.htm

26 Willow Brook 1910.

27 Morris 1909, Jewelry, p. 5.

28 Ibid., p. 7.

29 Willow Brook 1910.

30 Bury 1976, p. 98.

SOURCES AND FURTHER READING

Addison and Underwood 2015: Rhian Addison and Hilary Underwood, *Liberating Fashion: Aesthetic Dress in Victorian Portraits*, Guildford, Watts Gallery, 2015

Bennett and Miles 2010: Phillippa Bennett and Rosie Miles (eds), *William Morris in the Twenty-First Century*, Oxford, Peter Lang, 2010

Berrow 1989: Jim Berrow, producer, 'May Morris: the art of decorative embroidery', *Contrasts IX*, Central Television, Birmingham, 21 July 1989

Breakspear 1983: Marjorie Breakspear, 'My Memories of Kelmscott', *Journal of the William Morris Society*, 5:3 (Summer 1983), pp. 8–15

Breeze and Wild 1981: George Breeze and Glennys Wild, *Arthur and Georgie Gaskin*, exh. cat., Birmingham, Birmingham Museums and Art Gallery, 1981

Browne, Davies, Michael and Zöschg 2016: Clare Browne, Glyn Davies and M. A. Michael, with Michaela Zöschg, *English Medieval Embroidery: Opus Anglicanum*, New Haven, Yale University Press in association with the Victoria and Albert Museum, 2016

Bryson and Troxell 1976: John Bryson (ed.) in association with Janet Camp Troxell, *Dante Gabriel Rossetti and Jane Morris: Their Correspondence*, Oxford, Clarendon Press, 1976

Bury 1976: Shirley Bury, 'Rossetti and his jewellery', *Burlington Magazine*, 118:875 (February 1976), pp. 94–102

Bury 1991: Shirley Bury, *Jewellery 1789–1910: The International Era, Vol. 2, 1862–1910*, Woodbridge, Antique Collectors Club, 1991

Calhoun 2015: Ann Calhoun, *Arts & Crafts Design: like yet not like nature – sources for a New Zealand Story*, New Zealand, 2015, www.artsandcraftsnz.co.nz uploads/9/8/3/5/9835758/artandcraftsnz_2015.pdf

Callen 1979: Anthea Callen, *Angel in the Studio: Women in the Arts and Crafts Movement, 1870–1914*, London, Astragal Books, 1979

Calvert 2012: Robyne Erica Calvert, 'Fashioning the artist: artistic dress in Victorian Britain 1848–1900', PhD thesis, University of Glasgow, 2012, http://theses.gla.ac.uk/3279/

Carlano 1993: Marianne Carlano, 'May Morris in context: British artistic needlework and its influence on European embroidery 1862–1902', in Marianne Carlano and Nicola J. Shilliam, *Early Modern Textiles: From Arts and Crafts to Art Deco*, exh. cat., Boston, Museum of Fine Arts, 1993

Carruthers 2013: Annette Carruthers, *The Arts and Crafts Movement in Scotland: A History*, New Haven, Yale University Press, 2013

Cheltenham: Cheltenham Arts and Crafts Museum, online exhibition, *May Morris – William Morris's Talented Daughter*, www.artsandcraftsmuseum.org.uk

Cobden-Sanderson 1926: Richard Cobden-Sanderson (ed.), *The Journals of Thomas James Cobden-Sanderson, 1879–1922*, 2 vols, London, 1926

Crane 1905: Walter Crane, 'Of the Arts and Crafts Movement', *Ideals in Art: Papers Theoretical, Practical, Critical*, London, G. Bell & Sons, 1905

Crane 1911: Walter Crane, *William Morris to Whistler: Papers and Addresses on Art and Craft and the Commonweal*, London, G. Bell & Sons, 1911

Cunnington 1970: C. W. and P. Cunnington, *Handbook of English Costume in the Sixteenth Century*, London, Faber & Faber, 1970

Davenport 1894: Cyril Davenport, 'English embroidered book covers', *The Studio*, 2:12 (March 1894), pp. 208–12

Davenport 1899: Cyril Davenport, *English Embroidered Bookbindings*, London, Kegan Paul, Trench, Trübner & Co., 1899

Delaware Art Museum 2010: 'A Belief in the Power of Beauty: a selection of work by May Morris', exhibition checklist, Delaware Art Museum, Wilmington, DE, 2010–11

Dickens 1879: Charles Dickens, *Dickens's Dictionary of London, 1879: An Unconventional Handbook*, London, 1879

Du Bois 1892: Henri Pène du Bois, *Four Private Libraries of New York*, New York, Duprat & Co., 1892

Duff and Prideaux 1891: Edward G. Duff and Sarah T. Prideaux, *Exhibition of Bookbindings*, London, Burlington Fine Arts Club, 1891

Fielding 1968: Una Fielding, 'Memories of May Morris 1923–1938', *Journal of the William Morris Society*, 2:3 (Winter 1968), pp. 2–5

Fredeman 2010: W. E. Fredeman (ed.), *The Correspondence of Dante Gabriel Rossetti*, vol. 9, Cambridge, D. S. Brewer, 2010

Gere 1975: Charlotte Gere, *American & European Jewelry, 1830–1914*, London, Heinemann, 1975

Gere and Rudoe 2010: Charlotte Gere and Judy Rudoe, *Jewellery in the Age of Queen Victoria: A Mirror to the World*, London, British Museum Press, 2010

Glaister 1880: Elizabeth Glaister, *Needlework*, London, Macmillan & Co., 1880

Godwin 2015: Joscelyn Godwin (ed.), *The Starlight Years: Love and War at Kelmscott Manor 1940–1948*, Wimborne Minster, Dorset, Dovecote Press, 2015

Gordon 1900: Ishbel Gordon, Marchioness of Aberdeen and Temair (ed.), *The International Congress of Women of 1899*, London, T. F. Unwin, 1900

Greensted 2017: Mary Greensted, 'May Morris and Ernest Gimson: a wartime relationship', in Hulse 2017

Harvey and Press: Charles Harvey and Jon Press, *William Morris: Design and Enterprise in Victorian Britain*, Manchester, Manchester University Press, 1991

Haslam 2016: Kathy Haslam, 'The Homestead and the Forest cot quilt', *William Morris Society Magazine* (Spring 2016), pp. 3–5

Higgin 2010: Letitia Higgin (with an introductory essay by Lynn Hulse), *Royal School of Needlework Handbook of Embroidery (1880)*,

facsimile edition, East Molesey, Royal School of Needlework, 2010

Hoban 2014: Sally Hoban, 'The Birmingham Municipal School of Art and opportunities for women's paid work in the Arts and Crafts Movement 1885–1914', PhD thesis, University of Birmingham, 2014: http://etheses.bham.ac.uk/5124/1/Hoban14PhD.pdf

Hobbs & Chambers 1939: Hobbs & Chambers Auctioneers, 'Sale of a large portion of the furnishings and effects removed from Kelmscott Manor', 19–20 July 1939

Holmes 2014: Rachel Holmes, *Eleanor Marx: A Life*, London, Bloomsbury, 2014

Horton 1982: Margaret Horton, 'A visit to May Morris', *Journal of the William Morris Society*, 5:2 (Winter 1982), pp. 14–19

Hulse 2017: Lynn Hulse (ed.), *May Morris: New Perspectives. Proceedings of the May Morris Conference Held at the William Morris Gallery, May 2016*, London, Friends of the William Morris Gallery, 2017

Jonsdottir 1986: Gudrun Jonsdottir, 'May Morris and Miss Lobb in Iceland', *Journal of the William Morris Society*, 7:1 (Autumn 1986), pp. 17–20

Kelvin 1996: Norman Kelvin (ed.), *The Collected Letters of William Morris*, 4 vols, Princeton, NJ, Princeton University Press, 1996

Kremer and Mason 2012: Carien Kremer and Anna Mason, *William Morris in 50 Objects*, London, William Morris Gallery, 2012

Leary 1981: Emmeline Leary, 'William Morris and May Morris', *Embroidery*, Summer 1981, pp. 47–49

Lockwood and Glaister 1878: M. S. Lockwood and Elizabeth Glaister, *Art Embroidery: A Treatise on the Revived Practice of Decorative Needlework*, London, Marcus Ward & Co., 1878

Londraville 1996: Janis Londraville, 'A visit to May Morris in London: Excerpts from John Quinn's diary of 1911', *Journal of the William Morris Society*, 12:1 (Autumn 1996), pp. 25–28

Londraville 1997: Janis Londraville, *On Poetry, Painting and Politics: The Letters of May Morris and John Quinn*, Selinsgrove, PA, and London, Susquehanna University Press, 1997

Londraville 1999: Janis Londraville, '"Lady Griselda's Dream": May Morris's forgotten play', in Peter Faulkner and Peter Preston (eds), *William Morris: Centenary Essays*, Exeter, University of Exeter Press, 1999

MacCarthy 2010: Fiona MacCarthy, *William Morris: A Life for Our Time*, London, Faber & Faber, 1994 and 2010

Mackmurdo 1892: Arthur Heygate Mackmurdo (ed.), *Plain Handicrafts: Being Essays by Artists Setting Forth the Principles of Design and Established Methods of Workmanship*, London, Percival & Co., 1892

Manning 1980: Elfrida Manning, 'A visit to May Morris, 1925', *Journal of the William Morris Society*, 4:2 (Summer 1980), pp. 18–19

Marsh 1986: Jan Marsh, *Jane and May Morris:*

A Biographical Story, 1839–1938, London, Pandora Press, 1986

Marsh 2002: Jan Marsh, 'May Morris: ubiquitous, invisible Arts-and-Crafts woman', in Bridget Elliott and Janice Helland (eds), *Women Artists and the Decorative Arts, 1880–1935*, Aldershot, Ashgate, 2002

Masterman 1984: Elizabeth Masterman, 'May Morris: some notes for book collectors', *The Book Collector*, 33 (Summer 1984), pp. 163–78

Menz 1994: Christopher Menz, *Morris & Company: Pre-Raphaelites and the Arts and Crafts Movement in South Australia*, Adelaide, Art Gallery of South Australia, 1994

Moore 1933: T. Sturge Moore, *Charles Ricketts R.A.: Sixty-five Illustrations*, London, Cassell, 1933

Morris 1962: Barbara Morris, *Victorian Embroidery*, London, Herbert Jenkins, 1962

Morris 1888: May Morris, 'Chain-stitch embroidery', *Hobby Horse*, 3 (1888), pp. 24–29

Morris 1889: May Morris, 'Of embroidery', ACES, 1889, pp. 68–74

Morris 1890: May Morris, 'Of materials' and 'Of colour and colouring', ACES, 1890, pp. 92–100 and pp. 100–7

Morris 1893: May Morris, *Decorative Needlework*, London, Joseph Hughes, 1893; new edn, Morris 2010, London, Dodo Press, 2010

Morris 1893 [2]: May Morris, 'Of embroidery', 'Of material' and 'Of colour', in *Arts and Crafts Essays*, London, Rivington, Percival, & Co., 1893, pp. 212–23, 365–75 and 376–86

Morris 1898: May Morris, 'Lady Griselda's Dream', *Longman's Magazine*, 32, (June 1898), pp. 145–57

Morris 1899: May Morris, 'Coptic textiles', *Architectural Review*, 5:30 (May 1899), pp. 274–87

Morris 1902: May Morris, 'Pageantry and the masque', *Journal of the Society of Arts*, 50 (June 1902), pp. 670–77

Morris 1903: May Morris, *White Lies*, London, Chiswick Press, 1903

Morris 1905: May Morris, 'Opus anglicanum – the Syon Cope', *Burlington Magazine*, 6:22 (January 1905), pp. 278–85

Morris 1905 [2]: May Morris, 'Opus anglicanum II – the Ascoli Cope', *Burlington Magazine*, 6:24 (March 1905), pp. 440–48

Morris 1905 [3]: May Morris, 'Opus anglicanum III – the Pienza Cope', *Burlington Magazine*, 7:25 (April 1905), pp. 54–65

Morris 1905 [4]: May Morris, 'Opus anglicanum at the Burlington Fine Arts Club', *Burlington Magazine*, 7:28 (July 1905), pp. 392–9

Morris 1909: May Morris, 'Jewellery', lecture transcript, c. 1909, London, William Morris Gallery (S4.3.20)

Morris 1909 [2]: May Morris, 'Opus anglicanum', lecture transcript, c. 1909, London, William Morris Gallery

Morris 1909 [3]: May Morris, 'Pattern-designing', lecture transcript, c. 1909, London, William Morris Gallery

Morris 1917: May Morris, 'William de Morgan: recollections', *Burlington Magazine*, 31:173 (August 1917), pp. 77–83

Morris 1917 [2]: May Morris, 'William de Morgan's art', *Burlington Magazine*, 31:174 (September 1917), pp. 91–97

Morris 1936: May Morris, *William Morris: Artist, Writer, Socialist*, 2 vols, Oxford, Basil Blackwell, 1936

Morris 1973: May Morris, *The Introductions to the Collected Works of William Morris*, 2 vols, New York, Oriole Editions, 1973, reprinted from the *Collected Works*, 24 vols, London, Longmans, 1910–15

Morris 1882: William Morris, 'The lesser arts of life (a lecture delivered 21 January 1882)', *Lectures on Art Delivered in Support of the Society for the Protection of Ancient Buildings*, London, Macmillan, 1882, pp. 174–232

New York 1919: *Rare and Valuable Books and Bindings Collected by the late Samuel P. Avery*, The Anderson Galleries, New York, 1919

New Zealand 1906: New Zealand International Exhibition, Christchurch, 1906–07

NPG: National Portrait Gallery, *Later Victorian Portraits Catalogue, May Morris Designer & Craftswoman*, www.npg.org.uk/collections/search/personExtended/mp03188/mary-may-morris?tab=iconography

ODNB: Linda Parry, 'May Morris: Designer and Embroideress', Oxford Dictionary of National Biography, 1993 online; revised Jan Marsh, 'May Morris: Designer and Craftswoman', ODNB, 2004–16 online

Paris 1914: *Exposition des arts décoratifs de Grande-Bretagne et d'Irlande*, exh. cat., Palais du Louvre, Pavillon de Marsan, Paris, Avril–Octobre 1914

Parry 1983: Linda Parry, *William Morris Textiles*, London, Weidenfeld & Nicolson, 1983; 2nd edn, Parry 2013, London, V&A Publications, 2013

Parry 1983 [2]: Linda Parry, 'The revival of the Merton Abbey Tapestry Works', *Journal of the William Morris Society*, 5:3 (Summer 1983), pp. 16–22

Parry 1988: Linda Parry, *Textiles of the Arts and Crafts Movement*, London, Thames & Hudson, 1988; 2nd edn, Parry 2005: London, Thames & Hudson, 2005

Parry 1996: Linda Parry, 'May Morris, embroidery and Kelmscott', in Linda Parry (ed.), *William Morris: Art and Kelmscott*, Woodbridge, Boydell Press, 1996, pp. 57–68.

Parry 1996 [2]: Linda Parry (ed.), *William Morris*, exh. cat., London, Philip Wilson in association with the Victoria and Albert Museum, 1996

Partington 1921: *Echoes of the 'Eighties: Leaves from the Diary of a Victorian Lady*, with an introduction by Wilfred Partington, London, Eveleigh Nash, 1921, https://archive.org/details/echoesofeightiesoovictuoft

Phillips 1996: Clare Phillips, *Jewelry: From Antiquity to the Present*, London and New York, Thames & Hudson, 1996

Phillips 2008: Clare Phillips, *Jewels & Jewellery*, rev. edn, London, V&A Publishing, 2008

Poynter 1880: Edward Poynter, *Ten Lectures on Art by Sir Edward John Poynter*, 2nd edn, London, Chapman and Hall, 1880

Ramwell 2005/6: Julie Ramwell, 'May Morris embroidered binding', *News from the Rylands: The Newsletter of the Special Collections Division of The John Rylands University Library*, The University of Manchester, New Series, 3 (Winter 2005/6), p. 11

Rowbotham 2010: Sheila Rowbotham, *Dreamers of a New Day: Women Who Invented the Twentieth Century*, London, Verso, 2010, p. 175.

Sedding 1893: John D. Sedding, 'Design', in *Arts and Crafts Essays*, London, Rivington, Percival, & Co., 1893, pp. 405–13

Sharp and Marsh 2012: Frank C. Sharp and Jan Marsh (eds), *The Collected Letters of Jane Morris*, Woodbridge, Boydell Press, 2012

Shonfield 1987: Zuzanna Shonfield, *The Precariously Privileged*, Oxford, Oxford University Press, 1987

Sloan 1989: Helen Sloan, *May Morris 1862–1938*, exh. cat., Waltham Forest, William Morris Gallery, 1989

Soros and Walker 2005: Susan Weber Soros and Stefanie Walker (eds), *Castellani and Italian Archaeological Jewelry*, exh. cat., New Haven, Yale University Press, 2005

Sparkes 1884: John C. L. Sparkes, *Schools of Art: Their Origin, History, Work, and Influence*, London, William Clowes & Sons Ltd., 1884

Swain 1980: Margaret Swain, *Figures on Fabric: Embroidery Design Sources and their Application*, London, A&C Black, 1980

Thomas 2015: Zoë Thomas, 'At home with the Women's Guild of Arts: gender and professional identity in London studios, c. 1880–1925', *Women's History Review*, 24:6 (2015), pp. 938–64

Thoresen 2012: Natasha Thoresen, 'The reluctant reformer: May Morris' United States lecture tour of 1909–1910', *Textile Society of America Symposium Proceedings*, September 2012, http://digitalcommons.unl.edu/cgi/viewcontent.cgi?article=1748&context=tsaconf

Tidcombe 1984: Marianne Tidcombe, *The Bookbindings of T. J. Cobden-Sanderson*, London, British Library, 1984

Tidcombe 1996: Marianne Tidcombe, *Women Bookbinders, 1880–1920*, London, British Library and New Castle, DE, Oak Knoll Press, 1996

Tidcombe and Middleton 1994: Marianne Tidcombe and Bernard C. Middleton, *Tregaskis Centenary Exhibition*, exh. cat., London, Designer Bookbinders, 1994

V&A 2011: V&A Museum, Stephen Calloway and Lynn Federle Orr (eds), *The Cult of Beauty: The Aesthetic Movement, 1860–1900*, exh. cat., London, V&A Publications, 2011

Walter 2010: Hilary Laucks Walter, 'Another stitch to the legacy of William Morris: May Morris's designs and writings on embroidery', in Bennett and Miles 2010, pp. 73–98

Weintraub 1986: Stanley Weintraub (ed.), *Bernard Shaw, The Diaries, 1885–1897*, 2 vols, University Park, PA, Pennsylvania State University Press, 1986

White 2017: Catherine White, 'Decorative needlework: May Morris and her embroiderers', in Hulse 2017

Willow Brook 1910: *Exhibition of embroideries and jewels: the property and illustrating the lectures of Miss May Morris, Feb 8th to March 12th inclusive...at the rooms of the Willow Brook Company, 124 East 25th Street, New York*

WMS 2012: William Morris Society, *May Morris 150th Anniversary Exhibition*, checklist, Hammersmith, London, 2012

CHRONOLOGY

1859	April	marriage of Jane Burden and William Morris
1860	June	move to Red House, Bexley, Kent
1861	17 January	birth of Jane Alice (Jenny) Morris
	April	Morris, Marshall, Faulkner & Co. opened for business
1862	25 March	birth of Mary (May) Morris
1865	Autumn	family move to Queen Square, central London
1871	June	Kelmscott Manor, Oxfordshire, leased as a holiday home
1873	January	family move to Chiswick
1874–76		attends Notting Hill High School
1875		business re-formed as Morris & Co.
1877–78		visit to Italy
1878		family move to Upper Mall, Hammersmith (Kelmscott House)
1878–81?		studies textiles at the National Art Training School, London
1881		visits Paris and sketches in the Louvre
1884		joins newly founded Socialist League
1885–96		manages embroidery department of Morris & Co.
1885–86		romantically attached to George Bernard Shaw
late 1880s		publishes occasional reports in Socialist journal *Commonweal*
1886		participates in private reading of Ibsen's *A Doll's House*
1887		engaged to fellow-Socialist Henry Halliday Sparling; performs in Socialist entertainment *The Tables Turned; or, Nupkins Awakened* by William Morris
1888		publishes 'Chain-stitch embroidery' in *Hobby Horse* magazine
1888–1931		exhibits at Arts & Crafts Exhibition Society shows
1890	14 June	marries Henry (Harry) Sparling; moves to 8 Hammersmith Terrace
1892		publishes 'Embroidery' in *Plain Handicrafts*
1893		publishes *Decorative Needlework*, publishes 'Of embroidery', 'Of materials' and 'Colour' in *Arts and Crafts Essays*; attends International Socialist Workers Congress in Zurich
1893–94		publishes 'Of church embroidery', 13 parts, *The Building News*
1894		separates from Sparling
1896		death of William Morris; relinquishes role with Morris & Co.; exhibits at the Society of Women Artists, London; visits Egypt with Jane Morris
1897		returns from Egypt
1897–1910		teaches embroidery at Central School of Arts and Crafts
1898		publishes *Lady Griselda's Dream*, one-act play
1899		divorce from Sparling; publishes 'Coptic textiles' in *Architectural Review*; joins the Society for the Protection of Ancient Buildings
1900		exhibits at Glasgow People's Palace exhibition of needlework

1902		visit to Orkney (Melsetter House)
1903		publishes *White Lies*, one-act play; visits Florence
1904		'Decorative art 1800–1885' in *Social England* 1801–1885, vol. 6
1905		publishes 'Opus anglicanum' articles, *Burlington Magazine*; joint exhibition with Katherine Adams at 33 Hertford Street, Mayfair
1906–07		exhibits at New Zealand International Exhibition
1907		founds Women's Guild of Arts
1909–10		lecture tour in North America
1910	8 Feb–12 Mar	exhibits at Willow Brook Company, New York
1911		cruise to Madeira and Morocco coast
1910–15		edits *Collected Works of William Morris*, 24 vols
1913		exhibits at Universal Exhibition, Ghent, Belgium; visits Mallorca
1914		death of Jane Morris; exhibits at Exposition d'arts décoratifs, Paris
1914–18		First World War
1915		commissions Ernest Gimson to design cottages and village hall at Kelmscott
1916		designs displays, Arts & Crafts Exhibition, Royal Academy; establishes Women's Institute, Kelmscott village
1917		meets Land Girl Mary Frances Vivian Lobb; participates in 'Problems of Reconstruction' symposium
1918		starts weaving tapestry at Kelmscott Manor
1919		'Weaving and textile crafts' in *Handicrafts and Reconstruction*
1921		writes preface to *William Morris and the Early Days of the Socialist Movement* by John Bruce Glasier
1923		moves permanently to Kelmscott Manor; 8 Hammersmith Terrace sold to Mary Annie Sloane
1924		first visit to Iceland
1926		second visit to Iceland
1927–33		fundraising for Memorial Hall, Kelmscott
1929		third visit to Iceland; exhibits at the Society of Women Artists, London
1930		camping trip, Outer Hebrides
1931		last visit to Iceland with Mary Lobb, Mary and Margaret Peirce
1932		exhibits at the Society of Women Artists, London
1934		centenary of William Morris's birth; opening of Memorial Hall
1935		death of Jenny Morris; contributes to exhibition of Cotswold Art, Cheltenham
1936		publishes *William Morris: Artist, Writer, Socialist*, 2 vols
1938	17 October	death of May Morris; burial in Kelmscott churchyard
1939	March	death of Mary Lobb
	7 July	Hodgson sale of books from Kelmscott Manor
	19–20 July	Hobbs & Chambers sale of furnishings and effects from Kelmscott Manor

CONTRIBUTORS

ROWAN BAIN
Principal curator at the William Morris Gallery, London, and formerly assistant curator at the Victoria and Albert Museum, London. She is the author of *William Morris's Flowers* (2019) and contributed to the publications *May Morris: New Perspectives* and *Shoes: Pleasure and Pain*.

HANNE FAURBY
Project curator of the exhibition 'Fabergé in London: Romance to Revolution' (2021–22) at the Victoria and Albert Museum, London, and co-editor of the book *Fabergé: Romance to Revolution*. Formerly assistant curator at the Victoria and Albert Museum she specializes in nineteenth- and early twentieth-century design. Her research encompasses jewellery, textiles, fashion and embellishment with particular interest in materials and techniques of making as well as social-reform influences on the creative industry.

LYNN HULSE
Dr Lynn Hulse is a textile historian and former Visiting Research Fellow at the V&A specializing in art embroidery in the home, *c.* 1860–1914. She is a Fellow of the Society of Antiquaries and co-founder of *Ornamental Embroidery*.

JENNY LISTER
Curator of Fashion and Textiles at the Victoria and Albert Museum, London, specializing in the nineteenth century. She curated the exhibitions 'Mary Quant' and 'Grace Kelly: Style Icon', and contributed to publications such as *Silk: Fibre, Fabric, Fashion*, and *London Society Fashion 1905–25*. Her current research interests include discovering and promoting the work of forgotten nineteenth-century dressmakers.

ALICE MCEWAN
Dr Alice McEwan has a background in art and design history, and in 2016 completed a PhD at the University of Hertfordshire on the playwright, socialist and critic Bernard Shaw. The project was funded by the Arts and Humanities Research Council (AHRC) and the National Trust, and focused on artefacts at Shaw's Corner, the home of the playwright, now managed by the Trust.

JAN MARSH
Biographer and curator, author of *Pre-Raphaelite Sisterhood*, *Jane and May Morris* and biographies of Christina and Dante Gabriel Rossetti. She has also curated exhibitions on nineteenth-century art and artists, including 'Black Victorians: Black People in British Art 1800–1900', held at Manchester City Art Gallery and Birmingham Museum and Art Gallery in 2005. She is a former president of the William Morris Society.

ANNA MASON
Former curator and manager of the William Morris Gallery, London, winner of the Art Fund Prize for Museum of the Year 2013. She has also worked for the National Trust at Red House, and organized many exhibitions on Morris and his legacy. She is editor of *William Morris* (2022) also published by Thames & Hudson, and is currently editing the correspondence of May Morris with Dr Margaretta Frederick.

CATHERINE WHITE
Catherine White studied history of art at the Courtauld Institute of Art, London, and is now a researcher and freelance writer. She is writing a biography of May Morris.

PUBLIC COLLECTIONS

CONTAINING ARCHIVES AND WORK BY MAY MORRIS

7 Hammersmith Terrace, London

Art Gallery of South Australia, Adelaide

The Art Workers' Guild, London

Ashmolean Museum, Oxford

Bancroft Library, University of California, Berkeley

Birmingham Museum & Art Gallery, Birmingham

Birmingham School of Art Archive, Birmingham City University

British Library, London

Crafts Study Centre, University for the Creative Arts, Farnham

Cranbrook Art Museum, Michigan

Delaware Art Museum, Wilmington, DE

Embroiderers' Guild, London

The Grolier Club, New York

International Institute of Social History, Amsterdam

The John Rylands Library, University of Manchester

Kelmscott Manor (Society of Antiquaries of London), Oxfordshire

Leicester Museums, Leicester

Lisa Unger Baskin Collection, David M. Rubenstein Rare Book & Manuscript Library,
      Duke University, Durham, NC

Manchester School of Art Collection, Manchester Metropolitan University Special Collections

Mark Samuels Lasner Collection, University of Delaware Library, Newark, DE

Museum of Fine Arts, Boston, MA

National Museums of Scotland, Edinburgh

National Museum of Wales, Cardiff

National Portrait Gallery, London

Rhode Island School of Design Museum, Providence, RI

The Ruskin & Morris Center, Osaka, Japan

Standen (National Trust), East Grinstead

University of Aberdeen (Special Collections), Aberdeen

Victoria and Albert Museum, London

Wightwick Manor (National Trust), West Midlands

The William Andrews Clark Memorial Library, University of California, Los Angeles

William Morris Gallery, London

William Morris Society, London

The Wilson, Cheltenham Museum and Art Gallery, Cheltenham

The Women's Library, London School of Economics

ACKNOWLEDGMENTS

This publication is the result of collaboration with many colleagues, in the UK and internationally. Primarily, the authors wish to acknowledge the generosity of the Trustees and staff of the William Morris Gallery and the London Borough of Waltham Forest for their support for the exhibition on May Morris, this book, and the conference of May 2016, all initiated by Anna Mason.

The authors are particularly grateful to Dr Lynn Hulse, V&A Visiting Research Fellow, who contributed detailed technical knowledge and expert editorial advice. Sincere thanks also go to Tom Windross and Kathryn Johnson of V&A Publishing. We also appreciate the attention given to the publication by the team at Thames & Hudson.

The William Morris Gallery wish to thank Andrea Hall, Gary Heales, Roger Huddle, Carien Kremer, Kate West and all the lenders to the exhibition. The Friends of the William Morris Gallery have also provided essential encouragement.

At the V&A, many curatorial colleagues have given their valued support, particularly Christopher Wilk, Lesley Miller, Clare Browne, Richard Edgcumbe and Clare Phillips. We also thank Connie Karol Burk, Moya Carey, Sau Fong Chan, Juliet Ceresole, Max Donnelly, Kate Hay, Elizabeth James, Sarah Medlam, Victoria Platt, Suzanne Smith, Jennifer Wearden and Michaela Zöschg. Camilla de Winton transcribed the Morris & Co. embroidery Day Book, enabling us to access the information it contained more easily. We are also especially grateful to Joanne Hackett and Sarah Glenn of Textile Conservation, Joanna Whalley of Metalwork Conservation and Richard Davies, Robert Auton, Ken Jackson and Steve Woodhouse of the Photography department, and Mark Gardner, for their specialist expertise.

The William Morris Network, informally chaired by Jan Marsh, has provided a source of mutual support, knowledge and practical assistance. Helen Bratt-Wyton of Wightwick Manor (NT), Helen Elletson at the William Morris Society and Victoria Witty of Standen (NT) all responded to calls for help. We are especially grateful to Dr Kathy Haslam, Anooshka Rawden, Heather Rowland, Gavin Williams and Carole Wilson of the Society of Antiquaries of London (Kelmscott Manor), for accommodating many requests.

Above all, we would like to record our gratitude to Linda Parry, who has always shared her extraordinary knowledge about textiles with great generosity. Without her groundbreaking scholarship on Morris this project would have been inconceivable. Finally, each of the individuals listed below has provided answers to questions and emails, giving access to collections and archives, and supplying images. This collaboration has made producing this book an enjoyable and enriching experience. We hope it will provide an introduction to May Morris and promote future study of her work.

Mariyam Ali and Fiona Waterhouse, Birmingham City University; Meg Andrews; Dr Sonia Ashmore; Tessa Bain; Barbara Bieck and Meghan Constantinou, The Grolier Club of New York; Dr Nicola Gordon Bowe, National College of Art and Design, Dublin; Stephanie Boydell, Manchester Metropolitan University; Dr Rebecca Bridgman, Birmingham Museum and Art Gallery; Stephen Calloway; Annette Carruthers; Alan Crawford; Julia Dudkiewicz, Central Saint Martins; Rebecca Evans, Art Gallery of South

Australia; Dr Margaretta Frederick, Delaware Art Museum; Monica Grose-Hodge, The
Art Workers' Guild; Kate Irwin, Rhode Island School of Design; Stephen Jackson, National
Museums Scotland; James Joll; John Kendall; Dr Brenda King; Lorna K. Kirwan, The
Bancroft Library, University of California, Berkeley; Mark Samuels Lasner, University of
Delaware; Paul Liss, Liss Llewellyn Fine Art; Lynn McClean, National Museums Scotland;
Laura Micham and Jennifer Scott, Lisa Unger Baskin Collection, Duke University; Sarah
Nicol, Leicestershire County Council; Dr Caroline Palmer, Ashmolean Museum; Pamela
Parmal, Museum of Fine Arts, Boston; Dr Keren Protheroe; Julie Ramwell, The John
Rylands Library, University of Manchester; Paul Reeves; Vanya Sacha; Frank J. Sharp;
Dr Alison Smith, Tate Britain; Lore Troalen, National Museums Scotland; Paul Tucker;
Jean Vacher, Crafts Study Centre, University for the Creative Arts, Farnham.

PICTURE CREDITS

All V&A images © Victoria and Albert Museum, London

All WMG images © The William Morris Gallery, London Borough of Waltham Forest

69 Gift of Jenny Legoe 1998. Art Gallery of South Australia, Adelaide. 991A1. Photo © Art Gallery of South Australia

70 Gift of Joanna Simpson 1988. Art Gallery of South Australia, Adelaide. 881A1A

31, 34, 41, 42, 93, 98, 105, 118, 148, 150, 152, 154, 155, 156, 157, 159, 190 © Ashmolean Museum, University of Oxford

151 Courtesy of The Bancroft Library, University of California, Berkeley

122 Lent by Art & Design Archives, Birmingham City University

40 British Library, George Bernard Shaw Papers, Add. MS 50563, f.6 recto

44 The William Andrews Clark Memorial Library, University of California, Los Angeles

82 Collection of Stephen Calloway

9 The Cheltenham Trust and Cheltenham Borough Council

68 © 1999 Christie's Images Limited

126 Crafts Study Centre, University for the Creative Arts

133 Cranbrook Art Museum. Gift of George Gough Booth and Ellen Scripps Booth CAM 1955.402

16, 33, 43 Mark Samuels Lasner Collection, University of Delaware Library

153 The Grolier Club of New York

172, 173 Leicestershire County Council Museums Service

144, 145 Courtesy of Liss Llewellyn Fine Art, www.llfa.gallery

177 Estate of May Morris, photograph/Manchester Metropolitan University Special Collections

60 Farago Art Fund 85.200. Rhode Island School of Design Museum, Providence. Photography by Erik Gould, courtesy of the Rhode Island School of Design Museum, Providence

74, 75 In memory of J. S. and Sayde Z. Gordon from Myron K. and Natalie G. Stone. Inv.1983.160C. © 2016. Museum of Fine Arts, Boston. All rights reserved/Scala, Florence

76 In memory of J. S. and Sayde Z. Gordon from Myron K. and Natalie G. Stone. Inv.1983.160b. © 2016. Museum of Fine Arts, Boston. All rights reserved/Scala, Florence

94, 95, 96 © National Museums Scotland

186, 187, 188, 189 National Museum Wales

191, frontispiece © National Portrait Gallery, London

6 © National Trust/Brian Gornal

174 © National Trust/Sophia Farley and Claire Reeves

27, 134 © National Trust/Vanya Sacha

58, 100 101, 102 Private collection

46 Private collection/Bridgeman Images (1019)

149 Private collection. Photograph by Vanya Sacha

4, 7, 32, 85, 86, 87, 88, 89, 90, 91, 92, 106, 121, 129, 137, 138 © The Society of Antiquaries of London (Kelmscott Manor)

62 © The Society of Antiquaries of London (Kelmscott Manor). Photo Thomas Tomasska

3 Photograph courtesy of Sotheby's

71 State Library of South Australia, Adelaide. B 49700

158 Copyright of the University of Manchester

47, 65, 66, 107, 108, 115, 184 The William Morris Society

INDEX